D0880874

# Twelve Months of Monastery Salads

# Twelve Months of Monastery Salads

*200 Divine Recipes for All Seasons*

## Brother Victor-Antoine d'Avila-Latourrette

The Harvard Common Press
Boston, Massachusetts

THE HARVARD COMMON PRESS
535 ALBANY STREET
BOSTON, MASSACHUSETTS 02118
www.harvardcommonpress.com

Printed in the United States

*Library of Congress Cataloging-in-Publication Data*

D'Avila-Latourrette, Victor-Antoine.

  Twelve months of monastery salads : 200 divine recipes for all seasons / Brother Victor-Antoine d'Avila-Latourrette.

    p. cm.

  ISBN 1-55832-277-9

  1. Vegetarian cookery. 2. Monastic and religious life. I. Title.

  TX837.D235 2004

  641.8'3—dc22                                2003024061

Special bulk-order discounts are available on this and other Harvard Common Press books. Companies and organizations may purchase books for premiums or resale, or may arrange a custom edition, by contacting the Marketing Director at the address above.

10  9  8  7  6  5  4  3  2  1

BOOK DESIGN BY DEBORAH KERNER/DANCING BEARS DESIGN
JACKET PHOTOGRAPH BY KIM GRANT

# CONTENTS

*Acknowledgments  ix*
*Introduction  xi*

SALAD BASICS · 1

JANUARY · 7

FEBRUARY · 25

MARCH · 43

APRIL · 61

MAY · 79

JUNE · 97

JULY · 113

AUGUST · 133

SEPTEMBER · 153

OCTOBER · 175

NOVEMBER · 197

DECEMBER · 213

SALAD OILS, VINEGARS,
AND DRESSINGS · 229

*Measurement Equivalents  245*
*Index  247*

*A meal, however simple, is a moment of intersection.*

Elise Boulding

# ACKNOWLEDGMENTS

I wish to thank our friends in France and here in the U.S.A., especially my dear cousins Anne-Marie and Bernard Cazenave-Latourrette from Pau, France, who shared some of their favorite salad recipes with me. I also wish to thank Louise Seamster, Aaron Ancel, and Michael Centore, all from Vassar College, who collaborated and helped in so many of the monastery tasks, including at times typing and rearranging the recipes.

Last but not least, I am most grateful to The Harvard Common Press for wanting to do this book, in particular to Pam Hoenig, my editor, who worked endless hours to make this book a reality.

Habit de Vinaigrié

# INTRODUCTION

*For the ear tests words, as the palate tastes food.*
BOOK OF JOB 34:3

There was a time when both professional chefs and ordinary cooks looked at salads as a secondary dish on the menu, not terribly important to everyday cooking, something added to the meal only for special occasions, such as a feast or celebration. This has changed in the last few decades and we are all the better for it. The great interest that surged in the late sixties in a healthy, fresher, and more natural cuisine has done wonders to expand the scope and value of salad as a unique resource. Salads, rich sources of vitamins and minerals, are the prototype of what is considered healthful eating.

Main course salads, which artfully combine vegetables, fruits, seafood, cheese, grains, pasta, and meat, have become favorites during the hot weather months and beyond. People now savor and enjoy salads all year round. We have only to look at the trendiness of salad bars to see this. Some of the reasons salads are so popular are that they are easy to put together, there are endless variations to please every taste and palate, and they seem to always provide a wonderful contrast of flavors, textures, colors, and nuances. There are salads that can be prepared well ahead of time and others that can be quickly arranged at the last minute. If one finds one's fridge full

of leftover fruit and vegetables, one has only to think of salad and all these ingredients will find their rightful place in the salad bowl. There is a certain balance, a certain harmony in a well-prepared and -arranged salad, which gives it a unique appeal. All the ingredients seem to blend effortlessly, creating the perfect plate, full of delicacy and wonder.

Salads today are deeply appreciated by all, no matter where they appear in the meal. They can be the perfect starter, an attractive main course, or a delightful in-between or finish to an appetizing meal. I myself put great emphasis on the salad as a main course two or three times a week during the summer months, for besides simplifying the task of food preparation in the kitchen, the salad is a natural answer to a monastic diet that stresses the consumption of vegetables, grains, fruits, and less saturated fats.

Salads, like soups, have always played an integral role in monastic cuisine. Monastic cooking is well known for its simplicity, wholesomeness, sobriety, and basic good taste. These are principles that mark a certain approach to cooking and are reflected in the dishes concocted in monasteries. Both salads and soups are seen as perfect prototypes for these principles and are considered quintessentially monastic sorts of foods.

Monastic cooking relies a great deal on the seasonal harvest of our gardens, farms, and orchards. Monks know that nothing can compare with the freshness and excellence of the products grown within the confines of the monastic enclosure. Nothing is so deeply appreciated at the monastic table as a well-arranged, well-balanced salad, the end result of our own cultivation and the thrifty creativity of the monastic kitchen.

The salads presented in this collection tend to be basically vegetarian, thus adhering to the principle of the monastic diet as prescribed in the Rule of St. Benedict. Dairy products and seafood are allowed, and consequently are included in some of the salads you'll find within these covers. The immense variety of salad recipes in this book remains faithful to its monastic inspiration. (There are a few exceptions, like ones calling for luxury items such as caviar, which are included for the benefit of those who don't adhere to a strict monastic diet.) The recipes here exalt the values of health, nutrition, and refinement of taste. A salad, carefully prepared, is always an occasion for celebration.

*Bon appétit!*

BROTHER VICTOR-ANTOINE
SOLEMNITY OF ST. BENEDICT

# Twelve Months
## of Monastery
## Salads

# SALAD
# BASICS

The immense variety of salad greens now available in our gardens, in the supermarkets, and at local roadside stands can be overwhelming at times. With such diversity to choose from, one hardly knows where to begin. Each of the seasons provides its own harvest of delicious, crisp greens to tempt our appetites. Every season also brings new hybrid varieties, which provide their own intriguing flavors. The true connoisseur or well-trained chef knows that to create a magical salad, one must combine some zesty greens, such as arugula, with some milder ones, such as red oak-leaf lettuce, in order to achieve a delicious harmony of flavors. Mesclun is an example of a perfect blend of flavors, textures, and tenderness, hence its rich appeal.

In our small monastery, we cultivate an assortment of greens—about nine or ten of them—all year round, except during the deep winter months. The seeds come from France and the United States, and they always provide marvelous results for the monastic table. Here is a list of greens (some are actually red) that I like to mix or include in a salad.

Lolla Rossa: From France, this is available green or red, with a tender, mild flavor. It is perfect served alone or mixed with other greens.

**Butterhead lettuce:** This lettuce is relatively small, with a loose head and a delicate, buttery taste. The three main types are Bibb (also called limestone), Boston, and and buttercrunch.

**Romaine lettuce:** Particularly appealing because of its crunchiness, it grows easily in the garden and keeps well in the refrigerator. (I usually pick it tender from the garden, before it grows to full size.)

**Red oak—leaf lettuce:** A tender and colorful addition to the salad bowl, it is easy to grow in the garden, especially during the spring and fall months.

**Red leaf lettuce:** This is not the same as red oak-leaf. A larger plant, it is commonly found in supermarkets and known for its mild flavor.

**Iceberg lettuce:** This is very popular because of its crunchy texture, mild flavor, and long life in the refrigerator. I'm not terribly fond of it, though, and we don't cultivate it in our garden or use it in our recipes. I must confess, when we do have it, we feed it to our chickens, who like it very much.

**Mesclun:** This is a tender mixture of salad greens sown and grown together and harvested early, when they are mild and crisp. Its cultivation originated in Provence, and from there its availability has extended to the four corners of the earth. Mesclun is easy to grow in the garden.

**Chicory:** This coarse green is very crisp and mostly bitter in taste.

**Baby chicory:** Also known as frisée, this curly-leaf green is small in size and very popular in France, where it is known as curly endive.

**Escarole:** This is a broad, leafy form of endive, with a mildly bitter flavor. It is cold and heat resistant in the garden.

**Spinach:** There are several varieties; I prefer baby spinach for salads because of its tender texture and mild flavor. Spinach can get very sandy, so be sure to wash it thoroughly.

**Dandelion greens:** Considered a weed by most lawn-loving Americans, dandelion greens are a favorite among Italians. There are several varieties available for cultivation. I particularly like them sautéed and served a bit wilted in a salad.

**Watercress:** Usually found growing wild next to streams, watercress has a peppery flavor that is particularly appealing in a mixed salad. It is used often as a garnish.

**Belgian endive:** Called *chicon* in Belgium, this is a favorite among chefs. With a crisp texture and distinctive bitter taste, it is excellent served alone or mixed with other ingredients in a salad.

**Arugula:** Called *roquette* in French, it has a spicy, mustard-like flavor that is extremely appealing. We grow two varieties at the monastery: *Arugula salvatica,* a perennial whose seeds were brought by a friend from Venice, Italy, and simple arugula, which is an annual and much milder in flavor.

**Mâche:** This delightful, tender, mild-flavored green is similar in size to baby spinach. A favorite of the French and Belgians, it grows well in cold climates, often surviving heavy frosts.

**Radicchio:** A form of red chicory, it is very popular in Italy and among chefs. Shredded long and thin, it is often used to enhance a salad. Unfortunately, because it is not cultivated in the United States and must be imported, it is rather expensive in supermarkets.

**Green cabbage:** We cultivate both green and Savoy cabbage in our monastery garden and like to toss them in coleslaw and other salads.

**Red cabbage:** Often used in salads because of its color and crunchy texture, it's a nice addition to the bowl!

## USEFUL TIPS FOR SALAD PREPARATION

1. Always choose the freshest ingredients, in particular the greens and other vegetables. Use them promptly, so they retain their original texture and flavor.
2. Wash your greens well. Place them in a salad spinner and spin them dry. Don't let your greens get soggy, or they'll quickly go bad.
3. Add the vinaigrette or salad dressing just before serving the salad; otherwise the vegetables, especially the greens, will begin to wilt. A vinaigrette should always be prepared at the last minute before serving, and one must not hesitate to use one's clean hands for tossing the salad.
4. For a perfect mixed salad, a *salade mélangée*, compose it with a variety of textures, colors, and flavors. Blend all harmoniously!
5. When preparing the greens for a salad, tear them by hand rather then cutting them with a knife, which often causes wilting.
6. Choose quality ingredients to prepare the vinaigrette or salad dressing: extra virgin olive oil, good-quality vinegar—balsamic, wine, sherry, or another vinegar to your liking—fresh spices and herbs, and, whenever possible, sea salt, freshly ground pepper, and French mustard.

## TYPES OF SALADS

Salads have many uses, they come in numerous forms and shapes, and they have diverse origins. For the sake of understanding each particular salad, I have created some categories to place them all in a context. The idea of classifying salads gives each one its own niche, its own identity.

**Classic international salads:** These salads are well known around the world, for example, Indian Curried Lentil Salad (page 219), German Potato Salad (page 10), and Horiatiki Greek Salad (page 115).

**Rustic salads:** Inspired by the traditional rural cuisines of several countries, they include Pear, Endive, and Brie Salad (page 17), Mushroom and Arugula Salad (page 80), and Two Cabbages Salad (page 14).

**Exotic salads:** These salads combine sophistication, inventiveness, and refinement, for example Madagascar Date-Nut Salad (page 48), Mango Salad Piquant (page 112), and Fava Bean Salad, Egyptian Style (page 164).

**Creative salads:** These include such salads as Spartan Carrot Salad (page 66), Herbed Tofu Salad (page 215), and Transfiguration Salad (page 137); made with wild rice and chickpeas.

**Plain and simple mixed salads:** Basic everyday recipes, they include Monastery-Style Coleslaw (page 222), Tomato, Onion, and Mozzarella Salad (page 143), and Baby Beet, Potato, and Onion Salad (page 162).

**Pasta salads:** These are tried and true, right for almost any occasion. Among the many included, try Mint-Flavored Fusilli Salad (page 118), Rotelle in Spicy Napoleon Sauce (page 141), and St. Basil Macaroni Salad (page 168).

**Egg, cheese, and fish salads:** For a shot of protein, enjoy Salmon and Avocado Salad (page 52), Pesto-Filled Deviled Eggs (page 105), and Dutch-Style Egg and Cheese Salad (page 51), among many others.

**Italian salads:** Highlights of the Italian offerings include Arugula and Dandelion Salad with Roasted Pears (page 89), Roasted Sweet Pepper Salad from the Piedmont (page 220), and Artichoke Heart Salad (page 221).

**French regional salads:** The diversity of French cooking is represented in such dishes as *Salade au Roquefort* (page 77), Zucchini Salad, Basque Style (page 125), and Provençal Mesclun Salad (page 92).

**Saints' salads:** St. Benedict Salad (page 129), based on rice and cucumber; Regina Salad (page 147), made with lettuce and tomatoes; and St. Cecile Cauliflower Salad (page 210) are just a few of the recipes I have dedicated to saints. You'll find them in the month of their feast day.

**Fruit salads:** Orange, Apple, and Fennel Salad (page 227), Persimmon and Greens Salad (page 195), and Riviera Cantaloupe Salad (page 149) are refreshing examples of this collection, many of which can be served either as dessert or as part of a delicious breakfast spread.

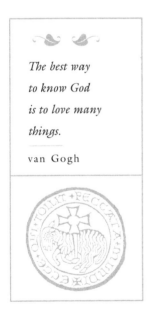

*The best way
to know God
is to love many
things.*

van Gogh

# JANUARY

Caesar Salad 8

Oriental Salad 9

German Potato Salad 10

Japanese Sprout Salad 11

Belgian Salad 12

Ancient Persian Salad 13

Two Cabbages Salad 14

Baby Spinach and Orange Salad 15

Boston Salad 16

Pear, Endive, and Brie Salad 17

Spicy Mixed Bean Salad 18

Frisée and Bleu d'Auvergne Salad 19

Capered Deviled Eggs with Beets
and Rémoulade Sauce 20

Monastery Deviled Egg Salad 21

Bar-le-Duc Salad 22

Orange, Apple, and Endive Salad 23

# CAESAR SALAD

MAKES 6 SERVINGS

## Croutons

¹/₄ cup olive oil

2 garlic cloves, minced

3 slices whole wheat bread, cut into 1-inch cubes

## Salad

1 head Boston lettuce, torn into bite-size pieces

1 medium-size head romaine lettuce, torn into
  bite-size pieces

1 medium-size red onion, thinly sliced

¹/₂ cup crumbled French or Danish blue cheese

¹/₄ cup freshly grated Parmesan cheese

## Vinaigrette

¹/₂ cup extra virgin olive oil

3 tablespoons red wine vinegar

1 tablespoon fresh lemon juice

¹/₄ teaspoon Tabasco sauce

1 teaspoon Dijon, Meaux, or another French
  mustard

Salt and freshly ground black pepper to taste

1 hard-boiled egg (optional), peeled and chopped,
  for garnish

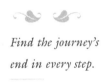

*Find the journey's
end in every step.*

Ralph Waldo
Emerson

1. To make the croutons, heat the olive oil in a large skillet over medium-high heat. Add the garlic and stir well once. Immediately add the bread cubes and cook, stirring, until they are lightly browned on all sides. Remove the croutons from the skillet and set aside.

2. To assemble the salad, put the greens and onion in a deep salad bowl. Add the blue cheese and Parmesan and toss gently to mix.

3. Whisk the vinaigrette ingredients together in a measuring cup or small bowl until thickened. Pour over the salad and toss gently to coat. Add the croutons and chopped egg, if using, and toss once more. Serve immediately.

# ORIENTAL SALAD

### Dressing

$^1/_3$ cup sunflower oil or another vegetable oil

1 tablespoon sesame oil

1 teaspoon soy sauce

2 tablespoons fresh lemon juice

1 teaspoon cider vinegar

1 tablespoon honey

Salt and freshly ground black pepper to taste

### Salad

1 cup fresh bean sprouts, rinsed with boiling water
and patted dry

1 bunch watercress, stems trimmed off, and torn
into bite-size pieces

1 head Boston lettuce, torn into bite-size pieces

1 medium-size or large sweet apple, peeled, cored,
and thinly sliced

3 scallions, finely chopped

Handful of lightly cooked snow peas

A few cooked shrimp (optional)

1. Whisk the dressing ingredients together in a measuring cup or small bowl
   until thickened. Refrigerate for at least 2 hours before serving to allow the
   flavors to develop.
2. Put the salad ingredients in a large salad bowl. Just before serving, pour the
   dressing over everything and toss lightly to coat. Serve immediately.

*January*

# GERMAN POTATO SALAD

*Salad*

10 medium-size red potatoes

2 large cucumbers, peeled, quartered lengthwise, seeded, and cubed

1 medium-size Vidalia onion, finely chopped

1 dill pickle, cubed

*Dressing*

3 tablespoons mayonnaise (store-bought is fine)

2 tablespoons Dijon, Meaux, or another French mustard

$1/2$ cup olive oil

$1/4$ cup cider vinegar

Salt and freshly ground black pepper to taste

$1/3$ cup finely chopped fresh Italian parsley for garnish

*He that drinks not wine after salad is in danger to get sick.*

English proverb

1. To make the salad, cook the potatoes in a large saucepan of boiling salted water until just tender when pierced with a sharp knife; start checking after 10 to 15 minutes of cooking. Do not overcook them. Drain, then rinse under cold running water. Let them stand for a few minute until they cool off. Peel, then slice the potatotes $1/4$ inch thick and put them in a large salad bowl. Add the cucumber, onion, and pickle and toss lightly so as not to break up the potato slices.

2. Combine the dressing ingredients in a blender and whirl until smooth. Pour over the salad and toss gently to coat everything.

3. Just before serving, sprinkle the chopped parsley over the salad. Serve at room temperature.

# Japanese Sprout Salad

### Dressing

⅓ cup sunflower oil or another vegetable oil

1 tablespoon sesame oil

1 tablespoon soy sauce

1 tablespoon white wine vinegar

2 teaspoons honey

### Salad

1 pound fresh bean sprouts, rinsed with boiling water and patted dry

4 scallions, finely chopped

1 bunch watercress, stems trimmed off, and torn into bite-size pieces

1 medium-size red bell pepper, seeded and finely chopped or diced

1. Whisk the dressing ingredients together in a measuring cup or small bowl until thickened. Refrigerate for at least 2 hours to allow the flavors to develop. Whisk once more before using.
2. To assemble the salad, put the bean sprouts in a salad bowl. Add the scallions, watercress, and red pepper.
3. Just before serving, pour the dressing over everything and toss lightly to coat. Serve immediately.

# BELGIAN SALAD

## Salad

4 medium-size Belgian endives, separated into leaves

1 large bunch watercress, stems trimmed off

2 navel oranges, peeled, with white pith removed, sliced into rounds, and cut into small pieces

2 shallots, finely chopped

## Dressing

⅓ cup fruity extra virgin olive oil

3 tablespoons Raspberry-Scented Vinegar (page 236) or red wine vinegar

2 tablespoons mayonnaise (store-bought is fine)

1 teaspoon Dijon mustard

Salt and freshly ground black pepper to taste

2 hard-boiled eggs, peeled and chopped, for garnish

1. To assemble the salad, put the endives, watercress, oranges, and shallots in a good-size salad bowl. Toss lightly.
2. Just before serving, whisk together the dressing ingredients in a measuring cup or small bowl until thickened and pour over the salad. Toss gently to coat, sprinkle the chopped eggs on top, and serve immediately.

*With mind and body, we earnestly implore You in your goodness, to bless these various herbs and vegetables. Add to their natural powers the healing power of Your grace. May they keep off disease and adversity from the men and beasts who use them in Your name.*

Russian prayer

# ANCIENT PERSIAN SALAD

*he ancient Persians believed that watercress and spinach helped their children grow properly, so they used them frequently in their diet. There is probably some truth to this, since both vegetables are wonderful sources of vitamins and minerals. They frequently added chicken to the salad and it was then a whole meal for them. Here I substituted tuna for the diced cooked chicken in the original recipe, for those who don't eat meat and want to add some some protein to the salad. (When I prepare it, I use only vegetables.)*

MAKES 6 TO 8 SERVINGS

*Dressing*

1/3 cup extra virgin olive oil

1/4 cup fresh lemon juice

1 tablespoon Dijon mustard

1 garlic clove, minced

2 tablespoons finely chopped fresh dill

Salt and freshly ground black pepper to taste

*Salad*

1 bunch watercress, stems trimmed off and torn into bite-size pieces

1/2 pound baby spinach

2 large carrots, peeled and cut into matchsticks

1 onion, thinly sliced

1 medium-size cucumber, cut into thin rounds

One 6-ounce can chunk light tuna, drained

1. Whisk the dressing ingredients together in a measuring cup or small bowl until thickened. Refrigerate, covered, while you prep the rest of the salad, so the garlic flavor can develop.
2. Put all the salad ingredients except the tuna in a large salad bowl.
3. Just before serving, add the tuna. Whisk the dressing again and pour it over the salad. Toss lightly to coat and serve immediately.

# Two Cabbages Salad

*his salad may be prepared the day before it is eaten, for it improves with time and tastes better the following day. This is an all-seasons salad, perfect for any occasion of the year.*

### Salad

2 cups cored and shredded green cabbage

2 cups cored and shredded red cabbage

3 medium-size carrots, peeled and grated or finely shredded

1 medium-size onion, finely chopped

$1/2$ cup raisins

### Dressing

$1/3$ cup extra virgin olive oil

5 tablespoons cider vinegar

2 tablespoons orange juice

2 teaspoons sugar

Salt and freshly ground black pepper to taste

1. To assemble the salad, put the cabbages, carrots, onion, and raisins in a deep salad bowl and mix together well.

2. Whisk the dressing ingredients together in a measuring cup or small bowl until thickened. Taste and adjust the seasoning. Pour the dressing over the salad and toss, making sure the vegetables are well distributed and evenly coated. Put the salad in the refrigerator until ready to serve.

# BABY SPINACH AND ORANGE SALAD

*This is a refreshing salad to serve after a hearty main course. It is both light and appetizing, with a lovely, creamy taste.*

MAKES 6 TO 8 SERVINGS

$^1/_2$ pound baby spinach

3 medium-size oranges, peeled, with white pith
   removed, separated into segments, and cut in half

1 small cucumber, peeled and cut into thin rounds

1 medium-size red onion, cut in half and thinly
   sliced into half-moons

$^1/_3$ cup walnuts, coarsely chopped and lightly
   toasted in a preheated 350°F oven

Honey Mustard Dressing (page 240)

1. To assemble the salad, put the spinach, oranges, cucumber, onion, and walnuts in a large salad bowl and toss gently to combine.
2. Prepare the dressing ahead of time. Just before serving, pour it over the salad and toss to coat. Serve immediately.

*What is the saint's reward? What ours after death?*
*It is the lily flower of purest godliness.*

Angelus Silesius

# BOSTON SALAD

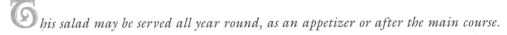

*This salad may be served all year round, as an appetizer or after the main course.*

MAKES 6 TO 8 SERVINGS

*Salad*

2 medium-size heads Boston lettuce, torn into bite-size pieces

2 medium-size ripe but firm avocados, peeled, pitted, and sliced

2 medium-size oranges, peeled, with white pith removed, and cut into rounds

1/2 cup pecan halves

2 scallions, thinly sliced

*Dressing*

1/2 cup mayonnaise, homemade (page 238) or store-bought

3 tablespoons pure maple syrup

2 tablespoons fresh lemon juice

2 tablespoons caraway seeds

1 teaspoon prepared horseradish

Salt and freshly ground black pepper to taste

1. Put all the salad ingredients in a large salad bowl and toss lightly to combine.

2. Whisk together the dressing ingredients in a measuring cup or small bowl until well combined. Pour over the salad and toss lightly until everything is evenly coated. Serve at room temperature.

*A bowl of fresh, tender leaves from any of half a hundred kinds of garden lettuces, unadorned except by the simplest possible mixture of oil, vinegar and seasoning, is a joy to the palate.*

M. F. K. Fisher

# PEAR, ENDIVE, AND BRIE SALAD

*he combination of the Brie and the pears gives a lovely warm flavor to this salad. It is best as an appetizer, but it can also be served after the main course, in anticipation of dessert.*

**MAKES 6 SERVINGS**

*Salad*

3 medium-size ripe but firm pears

2 medium-size Belgian endives, separated into leaves

6 ounces Brie cheese, at room temperature, cut into thin wedges

1 tablespoon butter

1/2 cup pecans, finely chopped

*Vinaigrette*

6 tablespoons extra virgin olive oil

3 tablespoons tarragon vinegar

Salt and freshly ground black pepper to taste

1/4 cup minced fresh chives for garnish

1. To assemble the salad, peel the pears and cut them carefully into quarters lengthwise. Trim the core away, then cut each quarter in half lengthwise. Put the pears in the salad bowl. Cut the endive leaves in half lengthwise. Put them in the salad bowl. Add the cheese and toss gently.

2. Melt the butter in a small skillet over low heat. Add the pecans and cook for about 3 to 4 minutes, stirring constantly. Remove from the heat and let cool for a few minutes, then add to the salad bowl.

3. Whisk together the vinaigrette ingredients in a measuring cup or small bowl until thickened. Pour over the salad and toss gently to coat. Sprinkle the chives on top and serve immediately.

# SPICY MIXED BEAN SALAD

*This salad can be prepared and served all year round and is a popular dish at parties and potlucks.*

MAKES 6 SERVINGS

## Salad

1 cup freshly cooked or canned black beans, drained and rinsed

1 cup freshly cooked or canned red beans, drained and rinsed

1 cup freshly cooked or canned white beans, such as cannellini, drained and rinsed

1 cup frozen or canned corn kernels, thawed and/or drained if necessary

1 medium-size red onion, finely chopped

3 garlic cloves, minced

1 medium-size red bell pepper, seeded and chopped

## Dressing

$\frac{1}{3}$ cup extra virgin olive oil

3 tablespoons white wine vinegar or fresh lemon juice

1 teaspoon Dijon mustard

$\frac{1}{2}$ teaspoon paprika

$\frac{1}{2}$ teaspoon ground cumin

Salt and freshly ground black pepper to taste

4 sprigs fresh cilantro, finely chopped, for garnish

*We are shaped and fashioned by what we love.*

Goethe

1. To assemble the salad, put all the beans in a large bowl (I like to use a ceramic one). Add the corn, onion, garlic, and pepper and toss together well.

2. Whisk the dressing ingredients together in a measuring cup or small bowl until thickened. Pour over the salad and toss lightly to coat. Refrigerate for 1 or 2 hours before serving.

3. Just before serving, sprinkle with the cilantro. Serve immediately.

# FRISÉE AND BLEU D'AUVERGNE SALAD

*This salad is best served after the main course. Since it combines fresh greens and cheese, there is no need to bring out more cheese afterward.*

MAKES 6 SERVINGS

### Salad

1 small head frisée (baby chicory), torn into bite-size pieces

6 ounces Bleu d'Auvergne or a similar blue cheese, crumbled

### Croutons

3 tablespoons olive oil

6 thin slices French bread, cubed

$1/2$ cup pecans, coarsely chopped

$1/2$ teaspoon garlic powder

### Vinaigrette

6 tablespoons extra virgin olive oil

3 tablespoons white wine vinegar

Salt and freshly ground black pepper to taste

1. To assemble the salad, put the frisée in a good-size salad bowl. Add the crumbled cheese and let it sit while preparing the croutons.

2. To make the croutons, heat the olive oil over medium-low heat in a medium-size skillet. Add the bread cubes and pecans and sauté, stirring constantly, for about 1 minute. Sprinkle with the garlic powder and continue to stir until the bread turns light brown, 2 to 3 minutes. (If need be, lower the heat.) Add the crouton-pecan mixture to the salad bowl and toss gently.

3. Whisk the vinaigrette ingredients together in a measuring cup or small bowl until thickened and pour over the salad. Toss to coat, and serve immediately.

*Hospitality consists in a little fire, a little food, and an immense quiet.*

Ralph Waldo Emerson

# CAPERED DEVILED EGGS WITH BEETS AND RÉMOULADE SAUCE

### Rémoulade

6 tablespoons mayonnaise, homemade (page 238) or store-bought

1 tablespoon Dijon mustard

Salt and freshly ground black pepper to taste

### Salad

4 medium-size red beets, peeled, cubed, cooked in boiling salted water until tender, 3 to 5 minutes, and well drained

3 tablespoons fresh lemon juice

4 hard-boiled eggs, peeled

2 tablespoons capers, drained and coarsely chopped

1 small onion, finely chopped

1. Whisk together the rémoulade ingredients in a measuring cup or small bowl until smooth. Refrigerate, covered.

2. To make the salad, combine the beets and lemon juice in a medium-size bowl. Mix well and refrigerate for at least 1 hour.

3. Meanwhile, slice the eggs in half lengthwise. Carefully remove the yolks and place them in a bowl. Mash them with a fork. Add the capers and blend together. Add $1/4$ cup of the rémoulade sauce to the egg yolk mixture and stir until well blended. Refill the egg whites with this mixture.

4. Just before serving, add the remaining remoulade sauce and the onion to the chilled beets and mix well. Place 2 egg halves on one side of each of 4 salad plates. Place a pile of beets on the other side. Serve immediately.

# MONASTERY DEVILED EGG SALAD

*his is an excellent appetizer to serve at any time of the year. It makes a complete meal when one wishes to eat lightly.*

MAKES 6 SERVINGS

6 hard-boiled eggs, peeled

1/3 cup mayonnaise, preferably homemade (page 238)

1 tablespoon Dijon mustard

Freshly ground black pepper to taste

Dash of paprika

1 bunch watercress, stems trimmed off, for garnish

1. Slice the eggs in half lengthwise. Remove the egg yolks and place in a medium-size bowl. Mash them with a fork. Add the mayonnaise, mustard, pepper, and paprika and blend together until smooth. Check and adjust the seasonings. Fill the egg whites with the yolk mixture.

2. Arrange the watercress on 6 salad plates in the form of a nest and place 2 egg halves in the center of each. Serve immediately.

*A meal reflects the gentle nature and warm heart of the cook. Of course, some of us are more clever with our hands than others. But if one does the best one can, a fine meal results, almost as if by divine grace.*

Soei Yonedi

# BAR-LE-DUC SALAD

*This salad is a good, healthy combination of fruit and vegetables. It is highly nutritious. Bar-le-Duc is the name of a town in the Lorraine region of France.*

## Salad

2 grapefruits, peeled, with white pith removed, and separated into segments

2 medium-size red apples, peeled, cored, and sliced into thin wedges

2 medium-size carrots, peeled and grated or finely shredded

2 Belgian endives, separated into leaves

1 shallot, finely chopped

1 tablespoon fresh lemon juice

## Dressing

½ cup low-fat sour cream

2 tablespoons mayonnaise (store-bought is fine)

1 teaspoon paprika

½ teaspoon ground nutmeg

½ teaspoon dry mustard

Salt and white pepper to taste

1. Combine the salad ingredients in a large salad bowl. Toss and refrigerate until ready to use.

2. Whisk the dressing ingredients together in a measuring cup or small bowl until smooth. When ready to serve, pour over the salad, and toss to coat evenly. Serve immediately.

*Since our monastic life consists principally in singing God's praises, then, everything around us must also sing. The monastery, the monastic land and all it contains must sing with fruitfulness, with the radiance of beauty, attuned to perfect pitch by silence.*

A contemplative monk

# Orange, Apple, and Endive Salad

## Salad

3 oranges, peeled, with white pith removed, separated into segments, and diced

2 apples, peeled, cored, and sliced into thin wedges

1 head baby chicory (frisée), torn into bite-size pieces

$\frac{1}{2}$ cup pitted black olives, drained and cut in half

$\frac{1}{2}$ cup green seedless grapes

2 tablespoons capers, drained

## Roquefort Mayonnaise

$\frac{1}{2}$ cup mayonnaise, homemade (page 238) or store-bought

$\frac{1}{2}$ cup crumbled Roquefort cheese

Salt to taste

Pinch of white pepper

1. In a large salad bowl, combine the salad ingredients and mix gently.

2. To make the Roquefort mayonnaise, in a measuring cup or small bowl, blend together the mayonnaise and Roquefort, mashing the cheese a bit with a fork and stirring until smooth. Check the seasonings and add salt and pepper if needed. Just before serving, pour the dressing over the salad and toss to coat. Serve immediately.

*January*

Habit de Vinaigrié

# FEBRUARY

Avocado and Egg Appetizer Salad    26

Savory Cauliflower Salad    27

Perugia Fennel Salad    28

Marinated Roasted Pepper Salad    29

Mayfair Salad    30

Waldorf Salad    31

Venetian Gorgonzola Salad    32

Copperfield Salad    33

Endive Salad with Blue Cheese    34

Wild Rice and Barley Salad    35

Jicama and Avocado Salad    36

Savory Potato Salad    37

Italian Winter Salad (Insalata Invernale)    38

Plain Leek Salad    39

Pickled Deviled Egg Salad    40

St. Scholastica Salad    41

Royal Fruit Salad    42

# Avocado and Egg Appetizer Salad

*his salad, as the name indicates, is almost always served as an appetizer, though it also makes a wholesome lunch or brunch dish.*

Makes 4 servings

### Salad

2 ripe but firm avocados, peeled, pitted, and thinly
  sliced lengthwise

4 hard-boiled eggs, peeled and quartered

2 medium-size Belgian endives, separated into leaves
  and cut in half lengthwise

4 lemon slices

### Dressing

$\frac{1}{2}$ cup extra virgin olive oil

3 tablespoons fresh lemon juice

2 teaspoons Dijon mustard

1 shallot, finely chopped

Salt and freshly ground black pepper to taste

1. To assemble the salad, divide the avocado slices evenly among 4 individual salad plates so the slices overlap and point toward the center of the plate. Arrange the hard-boiled eggs similarly in a decorative fashion. Fill the remaining space on the plates with the endive, evenly distributed. Place a lemon slice in the center of each plate.

2. Combine the dressing ingredients in a blender and whirl for a couple of seconds. Taste and adjust the seasonings. Just before serving, pour the dressing evenly over the salads. Serve immediately.

*All nature is meant to make us think of paradise. Woods, fields, valleys, hills, the rivers and the sea, the clouds traveling across the sky, light and darkness, sun and stars, remind us that the world was first created as a paradise for the first Adam.*

Thomas Merton

# SAVORY CAULIFLOWER SALAD

*his salad may be served at room temperature during the cold weather months, or it may be chilled in the refrigerator and served cold during the hot summer months. On occasion, I substitute homemade mayonnaise (page 238) for the vinaigrette, though I still add the mustard and season with salt and pepper.*

MAKES 4 TO 6 SERVINGS

### Salad

1 good-size head cauliflower, cut into florets

3 hard-boiled eggs, peeled and coarsely chopped

2 shallots, finely chopped

2 tablespoons capers, drained

### Vinaigrette

$1/4$ cup olive oil

3 tablespoons hazelnut oil

3 tablespoons white wine vinegar

1 teaspoon Dijon mustard

1 teaspoon chopped fresh or dried tarragon

Salt and freshly ground black pepper to taste

1. To make the salad, put the florets in the top of a double boiler set over simmering water, cover, and steam until tender, 15 to 20 minutes, or cook in a large saucepan of boiling salted water for about 5 minutes. Drain and allow them to cool.

2. Put the cauliflower in a good-size salad bowl and add the eggs, shallots, and capers. Toss gently to combine.

3. Whisk the vinaigrette ingredients together in a measuring cup or small bowl until thickened. Pour over the salad and toss gently to coat evenly.

# PERUGIA FENNEL SALAD

*his salad is usually served after the main course, as a way of cleansing the palate and helping with digestion before the dessert is served.*

**MAKES 6 SERVINGS**

## Salad

5 medium-size fennel bulbs, stalks discarded

1 medium-size red onion, thinly sliced

24 pitted black olives, drained

1 cup pecan halves, finely chopped

## Vinaigrette

½ cup plus 2 tablespoons extra virgin olive oil

¼ cup white wine vinegar

Salt and freshly ground black pepper to taste

Finely chopped fresh chervil for garnish

1. To make the salad, bring a large saucepan of salted water to a boil, add the fennel, and cook for 10 minutes. Drain, rinse under cold running water, and drain again.

2. Cut the fennel lengthwise into paper-thin slices and put in a good-size salad bowl. Add the onion and olives.

3. Toast the pecans in a small dry skillet over medium heat, shaking the pan often to keep them from scorching, until they begin to give off a roasted scent, about 6 minutes. Add them to the salad bowl.

4. Whisk the vinaigrette ingredients together in a measuring cup or small bowl until thickened. Pour over the salad and toss to coat everything evenly. Refrigerate the salad for at least 2 hours before serving. Sprinkle the chervil on top and serve.

*God hides things by putting them near us.*

Ralph Waldo Emerson

# MARINATED ROASTED PEPPER SALAD

## Salad

2 red bell peppers, cut in half lengthwise and seeded

2 yellow bell peppers, cut in half lengthwise and
seeded

2 green bell peppers, cut in half lengthwise and
seeded

3 garlic cloves, minced

1/4 cup extra virgin olive oil

2 tablespoons fresh lemon juice

1 medium-size red onion, thinly sliced

20 pitted black olives

## Vinaigrette

1/2 cup plus 2 tablespoons extra virgin olive oil

5 tablespoons balsamic vinegar

Salt and freshly ground black pepper to taste

Thinly shredded fresh basil leaves for garnish

1. Preheat the oven to 400°F or preheat the broiler. To make the salad, put
   the pepper halves, cut side down, on a broiler pan and roast or broil until
   blackened, about 15 minutes. Remove from the oven and place them in a
   brown paper bag. Close the bag, shake a bit, and let cool.
2. Carefully remove the peppers from the bag, peel off their skins, then wash
   under cold running water to remove any blackened bits. Pat dry with paper
   towels and place in a deep bowl. Add the garlic, olive oil, lemon juice,
   onion, and olives, cover, and place in the refrigerator for at least 2 hours to
   marinate.
3. Whisk the vinaigrette ingredients together in a measuring cup or small
   bowl until thickened.
4. On each of 4 salad plates carefully arrange 1 red pepper half, 1 green pepper half, and 1 yellow pepper half, leaving the center of the plate open.
   Place 5 olives in the center of each plate and distribute the onion over the
   peppers. Pour the vinaigrette evenly over the peppers, garnish with the
   basil, and serve immediately.

*February*

# MAYFAIR SALAD

*his* makes an excellent crunchy appetizer or a delicious plate to follow the main course.

## Salad

1 fennel bulb, stalks discarded and bulb thinly
   sliced

3 medium-size sweet apples, peeled, cored,
   and diced

1 celery heart, thinly sliced

3 small cucumbers, left unpeeled and cut into thin
   rounds

1/2 cup raisins

## Dressing

One 8-ounce container (1 cup) plain yogurt

3 tablespoons finely chopped fresh chives

2 tablespoons finely chopped fresh mint

2 tablespoons fresh lemon juice

Pinch of garlic powder

Pinch of paprika

1 teaspoon Dijon, Meaux, or another French
   mustard

Sea salt and freshly ground black pepper to taste

*Let us rejoice
in the Truth,
wherever we find
its lamp burning.*

Albert
Schweitzer

1. To assemble the salad, put the fennel, apples, celery, cucumbers, and raisins
   in a large salad bowl. Toss gently, cover, and refrigerate until ready to serve,
   at least 1 hour.

2. Put all the dressing ingredients in a deep bowl and blend thoroughly with
   a whisk or electric mixer. Refrigerate until ready to use.

3. Half an hour before serving, add the dressing to the salad and mix well to
   coat everything. Refrigerate and serve chilled.

# WALDORF SALAD

*Salad*

2 large celery roots (celeriac), peeled and cut into
matchsticks

¼ cup fresh lemon juice

4 apples, peeled, cored, sliced, and cut into long,
thin strips

*Rémoulade Dressing*

1 very fresh egg yolk

2 teaspoons Dijon, Meaux, or another French
mustard

¼ cup heavy cream or crème fraîche

½ cup extra virgin olive oil

1 tablespoon tarragon vinegar

Salt and white pepper to taste

½ cup chopped walnuts (optional) for garnish

1. To make the salad, cook the celery roots in boiling salted water for about
1 minute. Drain, then rinse under cold running water. Place them in a deep
bowl, add the lemon juice, mix well, and refrigerate for a couple of hours
until you are ready to serve.

2. Just before serving, add the apples and toss lightly.

3. To make the dressing, with an electric mixer, beat together the egg yolk,
mustard, and cream in a medium-size bowl until well blended. Then add
the oil gradually as you continue to beat the dressing until thick and
creamy; toward the end add the vinegar and season with salt and pepper.
Pour over the salad and toss until everything is coated evenly. If desired,
sprinkle with the chopped walnuts right before serving. Keep refrigerated
until ready to serve.

*February*

# Venetian Gorgonzola Salad

*This is an appetizing salad to serve after the main course.*

MAKES 6 TO 8 SERVINGS

## Salad

1 small head baby chicory (frisée), separated into leaves

1 small head radicchio, separated into leaves and quartered

1 bunch arugula, stems trimmed off

1 Belgian endive, separated into leaves and thinly sliced lengthwise into strips

2 tart green apples, peeled, cored, and sliced

$1/2$ cup chopped walnuts

$2/3$ cup crumbled Gorgonzola cheese (if you can't find it, use any other blue cheese, such as Bleu d'Auvergne)

## Vinaigrette

$1/2$ cup extra virgin olive oil

6 tablespoons Basil-Scented Vinegar (page 234) or vinegar of your choice

1 teaspoon Dijon, Meaux, or another French mustard

Salt and freshly ground black pepper to taste

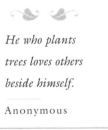

*He who plants trees loves others beside himself.*

Anonymous

*Twelve Months of Monastery Salads*

1. To assemble the salad, put the greens in a large salad bowl. Add the apples, walnuts, and cheese.
2. Whisk together the vinaigrette ingredients in a measuring cup or small bowl until thickened. Just before serving, pour over the salad and toss lightly, making sure all the ingredients are equally coated and well distributed. Serve on individual salad plates.

# COPPERFIELD SALAD

*Salad*

4 oranges, peeled, with white pith removed, and cut
   crosswise into 1/2-inch-thick rounds

3 medium-size ripe but firm avocados, peeled,
   pitted, and cubed

1 medium-size white onion, finely chopped

1/2 cup pitted black olives, drained

6 radishes, trimmed and thinly sliced

3 tablespoons fresh lemon juice

*Dressing*

1/3 cup hazelnut oil

1 teaspoon Worcestershire sauce

1 tablespoon cider vinegar

3 tablespoons honey

Pinch of cayenne pepper

Salt and white pepper to taste

1/4 cup finely chopped fresh cilantro for garnish

1. Just before serving, put all the salad ingredients in a good-size salad bowl.
   Toss gently, making sure the lemon juice coats everything.
2. Combine the dressing ingredients in a blender and whirl until well blended.
   Pour over the salad and toss again, making sure the dressing coats all the
   salad ingredients. Sprinkle with the cilantro and serve at room temperature.

*A Zen saying states that "flavor comes from the heart." Preparing food is
training for the spirit, and taking care to make food as delicious and
beautifully arranged as possible cultivates our aesthetic sensitivity. There is
no more splendid form of training.*

Soei Yoneda

# ENDIVE SALAD WITH BLUE CHEESE

MAKES 6 SERVINGS

## Salad

4 medium-size Belgian endives, separated into leaves and cut in half crosswise

2 tart apples, peeled, cored, and thinly sliced

1 shallot, minced

## Dressing

6 tablespoons walnut oil

3 tablespoons Spanish sherry vinegar (preferably Jerez)

1 teaspoon Dijon, Meaux, or another French mustard

Salt and freshly ground black pepper to taste

½ cup chopped walnuts for garnish

½ cup crumbled blue cheese of your choice for garnish

*Preach not to others what they should eat, but eat as becomes you, and be silent.*

Epictetus

1. To assemble the salad, put the endive, apples, and shallot in a large salad bowl. Toss gently and set aside.

2. Just before serving, whisk together the dressing ingredients in a measuring cup or small bowl until thickened, then pour over the salad. Toss gently, making sure all the salad elements are evenly coated. Divide the salad evenly among 6 salad plates. Sprinkle some of the walnuts and cheese on top of each serving. Serve at room temperature.

# WILD RICE AND BARLEY SALAD

*his salad is normally served at room temperature, but you can can also present it cold after refrigerating it for 2 hours. If you like, serve it as the main course for a light lunch or brunch.*

MAKES 6 SERVINGS

*Salad*

1 cup wild rice

$1/2$ cup pearl barley

5 cups water

Pinch of sea salt

$1/4$ cup olive oil

4 shallots, minced

3 celery stalks, thinly sliced

Leaves from 1 small bunch fresh Italian parsley
(4 to 5 sprigs), finely chopped

Two 1.5-ounce boxes golden raisins

$1/2$ cup blanched almonds, lightly toasted in a
preheated 350°F oven

*Dressing*

$1/2$ cup hazelnut oil

$1/4$ cup Spanish sherry vinegar (preferably Jerez) or
vinegar of your choice

Salt and freshly ground black pepper to taste

1 small head Boston lettuce (optional)

1. To make the salad, put the wild rice, barley, water, and sea salt in a large saucepan. Bring the water to a boil, reduce the heat to medium-low, and simmer gently until both grains are tender, 40 to 45 minutes. Drain and let cool in a colander.

2. Heat the olive oil in a small skillet over medium-low heat, add the shallots and celery, and cook, stirring, for 2 to 3 minutes maximum. Remove from the heat and let cool.

3. Place the rice-and-barley mixture, sautéed shallots and celery, parsley, raisins, and almonds in a large salad bowl. Toss lightly to combine well.

4. In a measuring cup or small bowl, whisk together the dressing ingredients until thickened, then pour over the salad. Mix until everything is coated well. If you wish, place 2 or 3 lettuce leaves on each salad plate and top with an equal portion of the salad. Serve immediately.

# JICAMA AND AVOCADO SALAD

*This enticing salad, full of the flavors of Mexico and the Southwest, is usually served as an appetizer, but it can also be served as a main course for a light lunch.*

## Salad

1 jicama (about 1 pound)

3 medium-size ripe but firm avocados

2 tablespoons fresh lemon juice

1 medium-size red onion, finely chopped

Leaves from 1 bunch fresh cilantro, finely chopped

## Dressing

1/3 cup extra virgin olive oil

2 tablespoons fresh lemon juice

Pinch of ground cumin

Pinch of paprika

Salt and freshly ground black pepper to taste

1. To make the salad, cut the jicama in half from top to bottom. Peel, then cut into cubes. Put the jicama in a large saucepan, add icy-cold water, and let stand for 30 minutes. Drain thoroughly, then put the jicama in a large salad bowl.

2. Cut the avocados in half. Remove the peel and pit, and cut into cubes. Place in a separate bowl, pour the lemon juice over them, and mix gently. This will help to protect their freshness and color.

3. Add the avocados, onion, and cilantro to the salad bowl.

4. Whisk the dressing ingredients together in a measuring cup or small bowl until thickened. Pour over the salad, toss well to coat everything, and serve immediately.

# SAVORY POTATO SALAD

*his salad can accompany a meat or fish entrée. It is usually served at room temperature, but if you prefer, refrigerate it for several hours and serve cold.*

MAKES 6 SERVINGS

## Salad

¹⁄₂ pound small new potatoes, peeled

1 cup shelled fresh or frozen peas, cooked in boiling
    water until tender and drained

1 cup diced celery

2 shallots or 1 small onion, coarsely chopped

2 small pickling cucumbers, such as Kirby, diced

## Dressing

¹⁄₃ cup extra virgin olive oil

¹⁄₄ cup tarragon vinegar

3 tablespoons chopped fresh dill or 1 tablespoon
    dillweed

3 tablespoons chopped fresh chervil

3 tablespoons chopped fresh chives

Salt and freshly ground black pepper to taste

1. To make the salad, cook the potatoes in boiling water to cover just until
   fork-tender, and drain. Cut in half when cool enough to handle.

2. Combine the potatoes, peas, celery, shallots, and cucumbers in a good-size
   salad bowl. Mix gently.

3. Whisk the dressing ingredients together in a measuring cup or small bowl
   until thickened. Pour over the salad and toss gently until everything is
   evenly coated. Serve at room temperature.

*My son, deprive not the poor of his living, and do not keep the needy eyes
waiting. Do not grieve the one who is hungry, nor anger a man in want.
Do not add to the troubles of an angry mind, nor delay your gift to a
beggar. Do not turn away your face from the poor.*

Ecclesiasticus 4

# ITALIAN WINTER SALAD

## (Insalata Invernale)

*Serve this salad as an appetizer or after the main course. As the name tells you, it is an excellent winter salad.*

MAKES 4 TO 6 SERVINGS

### Salad

1 medium-size head radicchio, shredded

2 medium-size fennel bulbs, stalks discarded and
   bulbs shredded

1 small bunch arugula, stems trimmed off

2 shallots, coarsely chopped

### Vinaigrette

1/3 cup extra virgin olive oil

5 tablespoons balsamic vinegar or wine vinegar of
   your choice

1 garlic clove, minced

Salt and freshly ground black pepper to taste

1. To assemble the salad, put the radicchio, fennel, arugula, and shallots in a
   large salad bowl and toss together well.

2. Prepare the vinaigrette ahead of time so the garlic flavor has time to
   develop. Whisk together the ingredients in a measuring cup or small bowl
   until thickened.

3. Just before serving, pour the vinaigrette over the salad and toss lightly,
   making sure everything is evenly coated.

# PLAIN LEEK SALAD

*Serve this dish at room temperature as an appetizer.*

MAKES 4 SERVINGS

8 good-size leeks

½ cup olive oil

¼ cup tarragon vinegar

Salt and freshly ground black pepper to taste

2 hard-boiled eggs, peeled and finely chopped, for garnish

1. Trim the leeks by cutting off the roots and the green tops. Remove the outer layer of skin. Cook the leeks in a covered double boiler in salty water for 15 minutes, or steam over 1 inch of boiling water, which will take a little less time. When the leeks are tender, drain and cool under cold running water. Drain them again and set aside.
2. Whisk together the oil, vinegar, salt, and pepper in a measuring cup or small bowl until thickened.
3. When ready to serve, place 2 leeks on each of 4 salad plates. Pour the vinaigrette over each serving and garnish with the chopped eggs.

*Acquire the art of detachment, the virtue of being methodical, and the quality of thoroughness. Above all, strive and pray for the grace of humility.*

Sir William Osler

# PICKLED DEVILED EGG SALAD

## Salad

6 hard-boiled eggs, peeled

1/3 cup mayonnaise, homemade (page 238) or
    store-bought

1 teaspoon Dijon mustard

2 tablespoons finely chopped pickles

Salt and freshly ground black pepper to taste

3 Belgian endives, separated into leaves

## Dressing

6 tablespoons extra virgin olive oil

3 tablespoons fresh lemon juice

Salt and freshly ground black pepper to taste

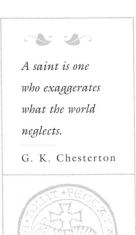

*A saint is one
who exaggerates
what the world
neglects.*

G. K. Chesterton

1. To make the salad, cut the eggs in half lengthwise. Remove the egg yolks and put them in a bowl. Mash them with a fork. Add the mayonnaise, mustard, and pickles and season with salt and pepper. Mix together until well blended.

2. Refill the egg whites with the egg yolk mixture.

3. On each of 6 salad plates, arrange the endive leaves on one side and on the other side, the egg halves.

4. Whisk together the dressing ingredients in a small bowl until thickened, and drizzle over the endives. Serve immediately.

# St. Scholastica Salad

*S*t. Scholastica was the twin sister of St. Benedict, and her feast is celebrated on February 10. It is one of those lovely monastic feasts that brighten our long, dark winters. Just as St. Benedict is considered the father of monks in the West, so is his sister Scholastica esteemed as the rightful mother of nuns.

**MAKES 4 SERVINGS**

### Salad

1 cup shelled fresh or frozen peas

1 fennel bulb, stalks discarded and bulb thinly sliced

12 cherry tomatoes, cut in half

2 shallots or 1 medium-size onion, chopped

1/4 cup crumbled Roquefort cheese

A few sprigs fresh Italian parsley, finely chopped

### Creamy Blue Cheese Dressing

1/2 cup plain low-fat yogurt

6 tablespoons extra virgin olive oil

2 tablespoons distilled white vinegar

1 tablespoon fresh lemon juice

1 teaspoon Dijon mustard

1/4 cup crumbled blue cheese (Roquefort or your own choice)

Salt and white pepper to taste

1. To make the salad, cook the peas in salted water until tender, 10 to 12 minutes if fresh. Drain the peas and allow to cool. Place them in a salad bowl. Add the fennel, tomatoes, shallots, cheese, and parsley and toss gently. Refrigerate until ready to serve.

2. To make the dressing, whirl the yogurt, olive oil, vinegar, lemon juice, and mustard in a blender until smooth. Pour into a small bowl, add the cheese, and mash it with a fork until the mixture is creamy. Season with salt and pepper to taste. Cover and refrigerate until ready to serve.

3. Just prior to serving, pour the dressing over the salad and toss until everything is well coated. Serve immediately.

# ROYAL FRUIT SALAD

$\mathcal{W}$e always serve this salad as a dessert.

## Salad

1 small ripe pineapple, peeled, cored, and cut into
    chunks
3 navel oranges, peeled, with white pith removed,
    separated into segments, and cut in half
14 fresh strawberries, hulled and cut in half
1 small ripe melon, seeded, cut from the rind, and
    cubed

## Dressing

½ cup orange juice
2 tablespoons fresh lemon juice
5 tablespoons honey

One 8-ounce container (1 cup) plain or vanilla
    yogurt for garnish
Leaves from 1 bunch fresh mint, finely chopped
    for garnish

*Sermons on diet
ought to be
preached in the
churches at least
once a week.*

G. C.
Lichtemberg

1. Combine the salad ingredients in a large glass salad bowl and mix together gently.
2. To make the dressing, whirl the orange juice, lemon juice, and honey together in the blender. Pour over the salad, toss gently to coat everything, cover, and refrigerate for 2 to 3 hours.
3. Serve the chilled salad on individual salad plates. Place 2 dollops of yogurt on top of each serving, sprinkle the mint over the fruit, around the yogurt, and serve.

# MARCH

GARDEN SALAD WITH *SAUCE AU CAVIAR*  44

ETRUSCAN SALAD  45

PINOCHE PASTA SALAD  46

PAPAYA AND ENDIVE SALAD IN RÉMOULADE SAUCE  47

MADAGASCAR DATE-NUT SALAD  48

EGG, CELERY, AND RADISH SALAD WITH TARRAGON SAUCE  49

BISTRO EGG SALAD  50

DUTCH-STYLE EGG AND CHEESE SALAD  51

SALMON AND AVOCADO SALAD  52

PARADISO SALAD  53

SICILIAN POTATO SALAD *(INSALATA DI PATATE)*  54

FARNESE SALAD *(INSALATA FARNESE)*  55

FRENCH MIMOSA SALAD *(SALADE MIMOSA)*  56

*SALADE PICARDE*  57

ST. JOSEPH SALAD  58

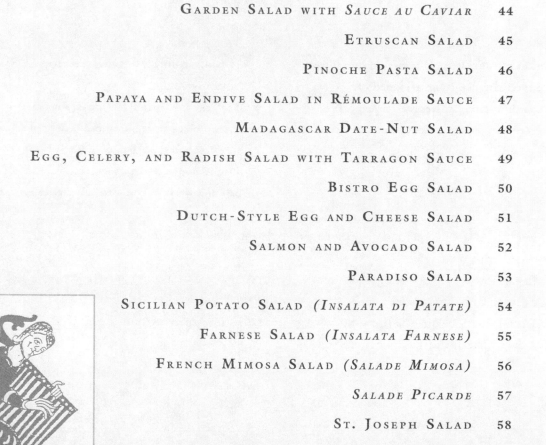

# GARDEN SALAD WITH SAUCE AU CAVIAR

*W*e usually don't eat caviar in the monastery. It is an unusual treat that a monk may enjoy on the rare occasion when he is invited to a special celebration outside his monastery, maybe once in a lifetime!

**MAKES 6 SERVINGS**

### Salad

1 head oak-leaf lettuce, separated into leaves

1 bunch arugula, stems trimmed off

1 bunch watercress, stems trimmed off

2 green bell peppers, seeded and cut into long, thin strips

### Sauce au Caviar

1/3 cup mayonnaise, homemade (page 238) or store-bought

3 tablespoons crème fraîche or sour cream

1/3 cup black caviar, or more if desired

1 tablespoon fresh lemon juice

2 tablespoons tomato sauce

Salt and freshly ground black pepper to taste

1. Put the salad greens and pepper strips in a large salad bowl and toss together to mix.
2. Just before serving, stir together the sauce ingredients in a measuring cup or small bowl. (This can also be done ahead of time and refrigerated for several hours.) Pour the dressing over the salad, toss it until everything is evenly coated, and serve immediately.

*Twelve Months of Monastery Salads*

# ETRUSCAN SALAD

MAKES 6 TO 8 SERVINGS

*Salad*

1 pound fusilli pasta

One 15.5-ounce can fava beans, drained and rinsed

One 6-ounce jar artichoke hearts, drained and chopped

4 scallions, coarsely chopped

1/3 cup fresh Italian parsley leaves, finely chopped

*Dressing*

1/3 cup extra virgin olive oil

1 tablespoon red wine vinegar

Salt and freshly ground black pepper to taste

1/3 cup grated pecorino cheese for garnish

1. To make the salad, cook the fusilli in boiling salted water until *al dente*. Drain, then rinse under cold running water and drain again, shaking the colander well. Put the pasta in a large salad bowl. Add the fava beans, artichokes, scallions, and parsley.

2. Whisk the dressing ingredients together in a measuring cup or small bowl until thickened. Pour over the salad and toss until well coated. Sprinkle with the cheese and serve immediately.

*Salads are the liveliest vegetables we eat. The chlorophyll in green things gives the body the greatest vitality and relays the sun's forces directly to the inner man. It is the green life-blood of the plant, the giver of strength and energy.*

Helen Nearing

# PINOCHE PASTA SALAD

*Salad*

1 pound penne pasta

10 oil-packed sun-dried tomatoes, coarsely chopped

2 cups shredded spinach

1 ripe but firm avocado, peeled, pitted, and cubed

1 medium-size red onion, thinly sliced

⅓ cup niçoise olives, drained and pitted

*Dressing*

½ cup plus 2 tablespoons extra virgin olive oil

1 tablespoon red wine vinegar

2 teaspoons fresh lemon juice

1 teaspoon Dijon, Meaux, or another French
   mustard

Salt and freshly ground black pepper to taste

Freshly grated Parmesan cheese for garnish

1. To make the salad, cook the penne in boiling salted water until *al dente*.
   Drain, then rinse under cold running water and drain again, shaking the
   colander well. Put the pasta in a large salad bowl and add the remaining
   salad ingredients.

2. Whisk together the dressing ingredients in a measuring cup or small bowl
   until thickened. Pour over the salad and toss gently until well coated.
   Sprinkle with the grated cheese and serve at room temperature.

# PAPAYA AND ENDIVE SALAD IN RÉMOULADE SAUCE

## Salad

3 medium-size ripe but firm papayas, peeled, seeded, and cut into matchsticks

3 Belgian endives, separated into leaves and cut into long, thin strips

2 small shallots, minced

2 tablespoons fresh lemon juice

## Rémoulade Sauce

6 tablespoons mayonnaise, homemade (page 238) or store-bought

1 tablespoon Dijon mustard

Salt and freshly ground black pepper to taste

1. To make the salad, cook the papaya matchsticks in boiling salted water for 2 to 3 minutes. Turn off the heat and let stand for about 10 minutes. Rinse and drain under cold water. Shake the colander or strainer and get rid of all the water. Put the papaya in a medium-size salad bowl, add the endives, shallots, and lemon juice, and toss lightly.

2. In a measuring cup or small bowl, whisk together the rémoulade ingredients until smooth. Pour over the salad and toss again lightly. Cover and place the bowl in the refrigerator until ready to serve, at least 1 hour. Serve chilled as an appetizer.

*The reward of a thing well done, is to have done it.*

Ralph Waldo Emerson

# MADAGASCAR DATE-NUT SALAD

*S*erve this salad as an appetizer over a bed of lettuce.

MAKES 4 TO 6 SERVINGS

*Salad*

4 celery stalks, finely chopped

1 cup chopped dates

4 apples, peeled, cored, and thinly sliced

2 medium-size red bell peppers, seeded and diced

1 long, thin cucumber, peeled, quartered
  lengthwise, seeded, and cubed

2 shallots, finely chopped

$^1/_2$ cup slivered almonds

*Dressing*

$^1/_4$ cup orange juice

2 tablespoons fresh lemon juice

2 teaspoons honey

1 teaspoon Dijon, Meaux, or another French
  mustard

Pinch of cayenne pepper

Salt to taste

$^1/_2$ cup plain yogurt

1. Combine all the salad ingredients in a large salad bowl and toss well to
   combine.
2. To make the dressing, stir together the citrus juices, honey, mustard,
   cayenne, and salt in a small saucepan over low heat until well blended and
   heated through. Remove from the heat and allow to cool. Pour the dressing over the salad and toss lightly to coat everything. Add the yogurt and
   blend everything thoroughly. Refrigerate for at least 2 hours before
   serving.

# EGG, CELERY, AND RADISH SALAD WITH TARRAGON SAUCE

*This is an excellent salad to serve at a buffet or informal party.*

MAKES 6 SERVINGS

### Salad

1 small head baby chicory (frisée)

3 hard-boiled eggs, peeled and coarsely chopped

3 celery stalks, thinly sliced

8 radishes, trimmed and thinly sliced

2 shallots, finely chopped

### Tarragon Sauce

½ cup low-fat sour cream

3 tablespoons fresh lemon juice

½ cup heavy cream or half-and-half

3 tablespoons chopped fresh tarragon

Salt and freshly ground black pepper to taste

1. To make the salad, tear the chicory into bite-size pieces and cover a large serving platter with them. Put the chopped eggs in a deep bowl, add the celery, radishes, and shallots, and toss lightly.

2. Put the dressing ingredients in a blender and whirl to combine. Pour the dressing over the egg mixture and mix until coated well. Spread the egg mixture evenly over the chicory and serve immediately.

*Of great use in the kitchen, and very pleasing and wholesome at the table, is the lettuce, an excellent supper salad, cooling and refreshing.*

John Woolridge

# BISTRO EGG SALAD

### Croutons

3 tablespoons olive oil

1 cup French bread cubes with their crusts

1 garlic clove, minced

### Salad

1 head romaine lettuce

2 shallots or 1 small red onion, finely chopped

3 plum tomatoes, cut into wedges

6 large eggs

### Vinaigrette

⅓ cup extra virgin olive oil

3 tablespoons tarragon vinegar

1 teaspoon Dijon mustard

Salt and freshly ground black pepper to taste

*One must summer
and winter with
the land and wait
its occasions.*

Mary Austin

1. To make the croutons, pour the olive oil into a medium-size skillet over medium heat. Add the bread and garlic and cook, stirring, until the bread turns golden. Remove the croutons from the heat and let cool.

2. To make the salad, tear the lettuce into bite-size pieces and put in a large salad bowl. Add the croutons, shallots, and tomatoes and toss gently to combine.

3. Break the eggs gently into a large saucepan of simmering salted water and let them poach for about 3 minutes. Remove them from the water with a slotted spoon, rinse briefly under cold running water, and drain. The eggs should remain soft in the center.

4. While the eggs are cooking, whisk the vinaigrette ingredients in a measuring cup or small bowl until thickened. Pour over the salad and toss gently. Divide the salad equally among 6 salad plates. Place 1 egg at the center of each plate. Serve immediately.

# DUTCH-STYLE EGG AND CHEESE SALAD

## Salad

3 medium-size to large beets, peeled, cubed, cooked in boiling salted water until tender, 3 to 5 minutes, and drained well

3 Belgian endives, separated into leaves and cut into 1-inch pieces

1/3 pound Jarlsberg or Gouda cheese, cut into matchsticks

4 hard-boiled eggs, peeled and sliced

3 shallots, coarsely chopped

## Dressing

One 8-ounce container (1 cup) low-fat plain yogurt

2 tablespoons Dijon mustard

3 tablespoons fresh lemon juice

3 tablespoons finely chopped fresh chives

Dash of ground cumin

Freshly ground black pepper to taste

1. To assemble the salad, put the cooked beets in a large salad bowl. Add the endive, cheese, eggs, and shallots and toss gently to combine.

2. Whisk the dressing ingredients together in a measuring cup or small bowl until smooth and well blended. Add to the salad and toss until everything is well coated. Serve immediately.

# SALMON AND AVOCADO SALAD

*S*erve *this as an appetizer or side dish or enjoy it as the main course for a luncheon or brunch.*

One 7.5-ounce can salmon, drained, picked over for
  skin and bones, and flaked

2 medium-size ripe but firm avocados, pitted,
  peeled, and cut into chunks

2 scallions, finely chopped

2 teaspoons capers, drained

$^1/_4$ cup fresh lemon juice

Dash of salt and freshly ground black pepper

$^1/_2$ cup mayonnaise, homemade (page 238) or
  store-bought

1 small head Boston lettuce, separated into leaves

1. To assemble the salad, in a large salad bowl, combine the salmon, avocados,
   scallions, capers, lemon juice, salt, and pepper and mix together well. Add
   the mayonnaise and toss until everything is evenly coated. Cover and place
   in the refrigerator until ready to serve.

2. Arrange 3 or 4 lettuce leaves on each salad plate. Place the salad on top of
   the lettuce and serve immediately.

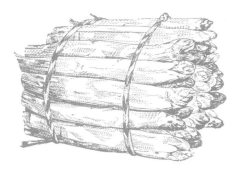

# PARADISO SALAD

*Salad*

1 head romaine lettuce, torn into bite-size pieces

$1/2$ cup croutons

1 small red onion, coarsely chopped

$1/4$ cup freshly grated Parmesan cheese

One 4.5-ounce package smoked salmon, cut into
thin strips

*Dressing*

$1/2$ cup store-bought Caesar salad dressing

2 teaspoons extra virgin olive oil

2 teaspoons fresh lemon juice

Salt and freshly ground black pepper to taste

1. In a large salad bowl, combine all the salad ingredients and toss until well combined.
2. In a measuring cup or small bowl, whisk together the dressing ingredients until well mixed.
3. Divide the salad equally among 6 plates. Pour the dressing over the top of each and serve immediately.

*What is more refreshing than salads when your appetite seems to have deserted you, or even after a capacious dinner—the nice, fresh, green and crisp salad, full of life and health, which seems to invigorate the palate and dispose the masticating powers to a much longer duration.*

Alexis Soyer

# SICILIAN POTATO SALAD

## *(Insalata di Patate)*

Serve this salad at room temperature or, if you like, refrigerate it for 1 hour and serve cold.

**MAKES 6 TO 8 SERVINGS**

### Salad

2 pounds small red potatoes, peeled, cooked in boiling salted water just until tender, drained, and quartered

1 celery heart, finely chopped

1 red onion, finely chopped

1 cup black Sicilian olives, drained, pitted, and chopped

$1/4$ cup capers, drained

1 gherkin (optional), finely chopped

A few sprigs fresh Italian parsley, finely chopped

### Vinaigrette

$1/3$ cup Sicilian or other olive oil

2 tablespoons dry Marsala wine

2 tablespoons red wine vinegar

Salt and freshly ground black pepper to taste

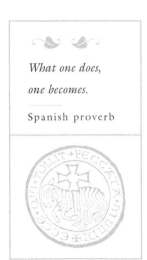

*What one does, one becomes.*

Spanish proverb

1. To assemble the salad, put the cooked potatoes in a deep salad bowl. Add the celery, onion, olives, capers, pickle, and parsley and toss lightly to combine.

2. Whisk the vinaigrette ingredients together in a measuring cup or small bowl until thickened, then pour over the salad. Toss lightly, making sure all the salad ingredients are evenly distributed and coated.

# FARNESE SALAD

## (Insalata Farnese)

The Farnese family was an old Italian noble family that possessed an elegant mansion in the center of Rome, today the location of the French embassy and a prestigious library. The piazza surrounding the mansion, Piazza Farnese, is the site of a famous outdoor farmer's market.

This salad is usually served as an appetizer during the cold weather months, when fresh greens from the garden are lacking.

**MAKES 6 TO 8 SERVINGS**

*Salad*

2 medium-size fennel bulbs, stalks discarded and
   bulbs sliced

2 medium-size Belgian endives, separated into leaves
   and cut in half lengthwise

3 oranges, peeled, with white pith removed, and
   separated into segments

1 medium-size red onion, thinly sliced

1/4 cup chopped fresh Italian parsley

*Dressing*

1/2 cup extra virgin olive oil

2 tablespoons fresh lemon juice

2 tablespoons orange juice

2 teaspoons honey

Salt and freshly ground black pepper to taste

1. Combine the salad ingredients in a large salad bowl and mix well.

2. Just before serving, whisk the dressing ingredients together in a measuring cup or small bowl until thickened. Pour over the salad at the last minute and toss gently to coat everything.

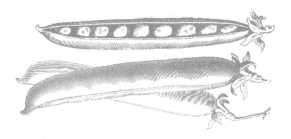

# FRENCH MIMOSA SALAD

## (Salade Mimosa)

*he mimosa blooms in France during the early spring, covering its branches with yellow flowers much the way a forsythia does. When the word* mimosa *is used in a culinary context, such as in this salad, it refers to the yellow yolk of an egg, used as garnish.*

MAKES 6 TO 8 SERVINGS

*Salad*

1 small head Bibb or other leafy lettuce, separated
   into leaves

1 small head baby chicory (frisée), separated into
   leaves

1 bunch mâche

2 medium-size Belgian endives, separated into leaves

1 bunch watercress

*Vinaigrette*

½ cup extra virgin olive oil

¼ cup tarragon vinegar

1 teaspoon Dijon, Meaux, or another French
   mustard

Salt and freshly ground black pepper to taste

3 hard-boiled eggs, peeled and finely chopped, for
   garnish

1. Do not cut or split the leaves of the greens; just get rid of the stems. Cover
   the greens with wet paper towels until ready to serve, and refrigerate them
   if it's going to be several hours. This keeps them fresh and crisp. Just before
   serving, arrange the salad greens in a large salad bowl.

2. Whisk the vinaigrette ingredients together in a measuring cup or small
   bowl until thickened. Pour over the salad and toss lightly to coat everything. Sprinkle the chopped eggs over the greens and serve immediately.

# SALADE PICARDE

*he name of this salad indicates that it originated in the ancient region of Picardie, in northern France.*

## Salad

1 small head cauliflower, cut into bite-size florets

1/2 head red cabbage, cored and cut into thin strips

1 medium-size red onion, thinly sliced

1 small cucumber, peeled, seeded, and cubed

1/2 cup chopped walnuts

2 hard-boiled eggs, peeled and chopped

1/2 cup crumbled Roquefort or another blue cheese

## Vinaigrette

1/3 cup extra virgin olive oil

1/4 cup red wine vinegar

Salt and freshly ground black pepper to taste

1. To make the salad, cook the cauliflower in a large saucepan of boiling salted water just until tender, 3 to 4 minutes, or in the top of a double boiler, covered, over simmering water, about 12 minutes. Remove from the heat, drain, and rinse under cold running water. Dry and let cool.

2. Put the florets in a large salad bowl, add the cabbage, onion, and cucumber, and toss lightly to combine. Just before serving, add the walnuts, chopped eggs, and cheese and toss again.

3. Whisk together the vinaigrette ingredients in a measuring cup or small bowl until thickened. Pour the vinaigrette over the salad and toss gently until everything is coated. Serve immediately. (If you prefer, add the walnuts, eggs, and cheese after the vinaigrette instead of before. It is a question of preference.)

*Be not anxious about what you have, but about what you are.*

St. Gregory of Nyssa

# St. Joseph Salad

St. Joseph, the foster father of Jesus and husband of Mary, is called in the Gospels the "just man." He was virtuous and always obedient to the Lord's commands. He is celebrated in the liturgy on March 19 as a solemnity and again on May 1 as St. Joseph the Worker. As a humble carpenter, he is a model for and the patron saint of manual workers.

Serve this salad either before or after the main course. It is also sufficiently filling to make a light lunch.

MAKES 6 SERVINGS

*Salad*

1/2 pound baby spinach

1 small head radicchio, shredded

18 cherry tomatoes

6 hard-boiled eggs, peeled and cut into wedges

2 shallots, finely chopped

*Vinaigrette*

1/2 cup extra virgin olive oil

2 tablespoons tarragon vinegar

1 teaspoon Dijon mustard

Salt and freshly ground black pepper to taste

1. To assemble the salad, in a large salad bowl, toss together the spinach and radicchio until well combined and divide equally among 6 salad plates. Arrange the cherry tomatoes and egg wedges attractively on top. Sprinkle the shallots over everything.

2. Whisk the vinaigrette ingredients together in a measuring cup or small bowl until thickened and pour evenly over each of the salads. Serve immediately.

*From every point on earth we are equally near to heaven and to the infinite.*

Frederic Amiel

# SAINTS' SALADS

The monastic calendar, like the secular one, is repeated year after year. It waits for no one and always arrives on time. It is based on the seasons of the liturgy and provides us daily occasion to remember God's friends and our intercessors, the saints. No one should be surprised, then, that so many recipes bear a saint's name. This is completely natural to me, for each day I think of and pray to the saint whose memory is kept on that date. I keep continual company with the Mother of God and the saints, and I am inspired by their words and examples.

Someone once asked me if there was a special mystical meaning in my recipes that bear the names of saints. The person thought the recipe was the creation of the saint for whom it was inscribed. She was later mystified, and almost disappointed, by my simple response. I told her that there were many ways of honoring the saints and keeping their memories alive. One of my ways was to name recipes after them, so that others might think of and remember their legacies.

A few years ago, I was asked to give a talk and do a book signing for the benefit of a local library. After the talk, the library trustees invited me to supper in one of their homes. They were lovely people, and I thoroughly enjoyed their company. When the time came to sit at the table, they surprised me by serving a meal using my own recipes. As they served the salad, the hostess announced, "This is St. Joseph's salad." Everyone laughed, and someone asked who St. Joseph was and why I had named this recipe after him. The question was not very difficult to answer, for St. Joseph is very special to me. I began telling everyone that Joseph was Mary's husband and Jesus's foster father and that he is particularly dear to me because of his unfailing protection; the recipe was simply a way of saying "thank you" to him.

When it was time to leave, someone approached me and said, "Thank you for telling us about St. Joseph. I had never heard of him." When I finally arrived back at the monastery and entered the chapel to sing Compline, I gazed at the icon of St. Joseph with renewed love and devotion. It seemed like there was a special aura pulsing from the icon, as if the saint was trying to convey something to me. Perhaps it was a simple "thank you" for honoring his memory.

Habit de Vinaigrié

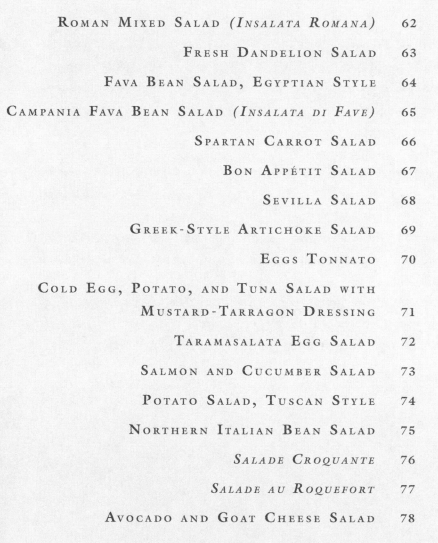

# APRIL

ROMAN MIXED SALAD (*INSALATA ROMANA*)    62

FRESH DANDELION SALAD    63

FAVA BEAN SALAD, EGYPTIAN STYLE    64

CAMPANIA FAVA BEAN SALAD (*INSALATA DI FAVE*)    65

SPARTAN CARROT SALAD    66

BON APPÉTIT SALAD    67

SEVILLA SALAD    68

GREEK-STYLE ARTICHOKE SALAD    69

EGGS TONNATO    70

COLD EGG, POTATO, AND TUNA SALAD WITH
MUSTARD-TARRAGON DRESSING    71

TARAMASALATA EGG SALAD    72

SALMON AND CUCUMBER SALAD    73

POTATO SALAD, TUSCAN STYLE    74

NORTHERN ITALIAN BEAN SALAD    75

*SALADE CROQUANTE*    76

*SALADE AU ROQUEFORT*    77

AVOCADO AND GOAT CHEESE SALAD    78

# ROMAN MIXED SALAD

## (Insalata Romana)

*Salad*

1 head red leaf lettuce

1 small head baby chicory (frisée)

1 bunch baby spinach

1 bunch arugula

1 bunch watercress

1 bunch dandelion greens

1 small fennel bulb, stalks discarded and bulb
   thinly sliced

4 scallions, thinly sliced

Leaves from 1 small bunch fresh Italian parsley,
   finely chopped

10 fresh basil leaves, finely chopped

*Vinaigrette*

$1/2$ cup fruity extra virgin olive oil

$1/4$ cup balsamic vinegar

Salt and freshly ground black pepper to taste

1. To make the salad, trim the stems from all the salad greens. Put the greens
   in a large salad bowl, add the fennel, scallions, parsley, and basil and toss to
   mix well.

2. Whisk the vinaigrette ingredients together in a measuring cup or small
   bowl until thickened. Just before serving, pour over the salad and toss
   lightly, making sure all the greens are equally coated. Serve immediately.

# FRESH DANDELION SALAD

*his is a good salad to serve after the main course. It is a great help to one's digestion.*

## Salad

½ pound dandelion greens, stems trimmed off

1 medium-size head radicchio, shredded

1 head green leaf or red oak-leaf lettuce, torn into
   large pieces

1 small head Boston or other butterhead lettuce,
   torn into large pieces

3 strips bacon (optional), fried until crisp, drained,
   and crumbled into small pieces

## Vinaigrette

⅓ cup extra virgin olive oil

5 tablespoons Raspberry-Scented Vinegar
   (page 236)

Salt and freshly ground black pepper to taste

1. To assemble the salad, combine the dandelions, radicchio, and lettuces in a
   large salad bowl. For nonvegetarians, add the bacon if you like.
2. Whisk together the vinaigrette ingredients in a measuring cup or small
   bowl until thickened. Pour over the salad, toss lightly, and serve.

*Each day is a little life; every waking and rising a little birth,
every fresh morning a little youth, every going to rest and sleep
a little death.*

Arthur Schopenhauer

*April*

63

# Fava Bean Salad, Egyptian Style

*Serve this versatile salad as an appetizer or main course for a festive lunch, or even for supper. Vegetarians tend to love this dish whenever it is prepared.*

MAKES 6 SERVINGS

### Salad

2 cups shelled fresh fava beans (from about 1 pound fava pods)

1 medium-size red onion, finely chopped

1 red bell pepper, seeded and diced

1 yellow bell pepper, seeded and diced

A few sprigs fresh Italian parsley, finely chopped

6 hard-boiled eggs

### Dressing

7 tablespoons extra virgin olive oil

3 tablespoons fresh lemon juice

1 teaspoon ground cumin

Pinch of cayenne pepper

Pinch of dried thyme

Salt to taste

1. To make the salad, cook the fava beans in boiling salted water until tender, 12 to 15 minutes. Drain, rinse under cold running water, slip the beans out of the skins, and put them in a salad bowl. Add the onion, bell peppers, and parsley and mix well. Peel the eggs, slice them in half lengthwise, and set aside.

2. Whisk together the dressing ingredients in a measuring cup or small bowl until thickened. Pour over the salad and toss lightly, making sure all beans are evenly coated.

3. Divide the salad among 6 salad plates and place two egg slices on each dish. Serve immediately.

# CAMPANIA FAVA BEAN SALAD

## (Insalata di Fave)

*Serve this salad as an introduction to a good meal.*

### Salad

2 cups shelled fresh fava beans (from about 1 pound fava pods)

1 celery heart, thinly sliced

1 small onion, finely chopped

$\frac{1}{2}$ cup pitted black olives, drained and coarsely chopped

6 fresh mint leaves, finely chopped

### Vinaigrette

$\frac{1}{3}$ cup extra virgin olive oil

2 teaspoons red wine vinegar

2 teaspoons fresh lemon juice

Salt and freshly ground black pepper to taste

2 hard-boiled eggs, peeled and chopped, for garnish

1. To make the salad, cook the fava beans in boiling salted water until tender, 12 to 15 minutes. Drain and rinse them under cold running water and slip off their skins. Put the beans in a deep salad bowl, add the celery, onion, olives, and mint and toss lightly to combine.

2. Whisk the vinaigrette ingredients together in a measuring cup or small bowl until thickened. Just before serving, pour over the salad and toss well to coat everything. Sprinkle the chopped eggs on the top and serve at room temperature.

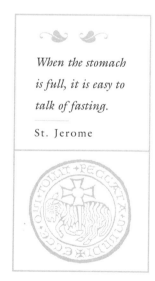

*When the stomach is full, it is easy to talk of fasting.*

St. Jerome

# SPARTAN CARROT SALAD

*This salad is usually served as an appetizer, and always cold.*

MAKES 6 SERVINGS

### Salad

6 medium-size carrots, peeled and grated or finely
   shredded

1 small head radicchio, finely shredded

1 small white onion, finely chopped

1/4 cup finely chopped fresh Italian parsley

### Dressing

1/3 cup extra virgin olive oil

2 tablespoons white wine vinegar

2 teaspoons fresh lemon juice

1 teaspoon honey mustard

Salt and freshly ground black pepper to taste

1. To make the salad, put the carrots and radicchio in a large salad bowl.
   Refrigerate until ready to serve. Just before serving, add the onion and
   parsley to the salad bowl and mix well.

2. Whisk together the dressing ingredients in a measuring cup or small bowl
   until thickened. Adjust the seasonings, if necessary. Pour over the salad and
   toss to coat everything evenly. Serve immediately.

*"Flavor comes from the heart" implies both cooking with one's whole soul
and giving thought to the right atmosphere in which to serve the results.
When care is paid not only to placing the dishes on the table but to cleanli-
ness and neatness of the room, the floral settings, and the arrangement of
food on the plates, the meal tastes twice as good.*

Soei Yoneda

# BON APPÉTIT SALAD

*This is a classic French salad that defies time and fashion, for it is always à la mode. As the name implies, this salad is an excellent starter to a good meal, stirring the appetite for other things to come. Of course, it can also be served after the main course.*

MAKES 8 SERVINGS

*Salad*

1 pound mixed salad greens or mesclun, torn into bite-size pieces

1 large carrot, thinly shredded

1/4 small head red cabbage, finely shredded

1 large green bell pepper, seeded and cut into long, thin strips

2 scallions, thinly sliced

*Vinaigrette*

1/2 cup extra virgin olive oil

5 tablespoons wine vinegar of your choice

1 tablespoon Dijon mustard

Salt and freshly ground black pepper to taste

1. Combine the salad ingredients in a large salad bowl and toss until well combined.

2. Whisk together the vinaigrette ingredients in a measuring cup or small bowl until thickened. Adjust the seasonings, if necessary. Pour over the salad just before serving and stir the salad to coat everything evenly. Serve immediately.

# SEVILLA SALAD

his refreshing salad is based on Seville oranges, which are appreciated for their sweet flavor.

MAKES 6 SERVINGS

## Salad

3 medium-size Seville oranges, peeled, with white pith removed, quartered, and seeded

1/2 pound baby spinach

1 red onion, cut in half, thinly sliced into half-moons, and pulled apart into strips

20 pitted black olives, cut in half

## Vinaigrette

1/3 cup extra virgin Spanish olive oil or another extra virgin olive oil of your choice

1/4 cup plus 1 tablespoon Spanish sherry vinegar (preferably Jerez)

Salt and freshly ground black pepper to taste

1. To assemble the salad, put the oranges in a deep salad bowl, add the spinach, onion, and olives, and toss until well mixed.
2. Whisk together the vinaigrette ingredients in a measuring cup or small bowl until thickened. Just before serving, pour over the salad, toss until everything is well coated, and serve immediately.

*Oh, green and glorious! Oh, herbaceous treat! 'Twould tempt the dying anchorite to eat: Back to the world he'd turn his fleeting soul, and plunge his fingers in the salad-bowl!*

Rev. Sydney Smith

# GREEK-STYLE ARTICHOKE SALAD

*S*erve this dish as an appetizer or as an accompaniment to the main course.

MAKES 4 SERVINGS

16 small artichokes

¼ cup fresh lemon juice, plus extra for drizzling

½ cup olive oil

1 bay leaf

4 sprigs fresh Italian parsley, finely chopped

Salt and freshly ground black pepper to taste

3 medium-size ripe tomatoes, peeled, seeded, and finely chopped

1. To prepare the artichokes, break off the leaves at the base and place each artichoke on its side on a cutting board. Using a sharp knife, cut the lower leaves off up to where the heart of the artichoke is found. Proceed to trim and cut off the leaves above the heart of the artichoke. Cut off and trim the rest of the leaves, following the same procedure, being careful to keep the heart intact. Using the knife or a spoon, scoop out and discard the choke. As you finish trimming each artichoke, put the hearts in a casserole dish filled with cold water and the lemon juice. Leave them for 30 minutes.

2. To cook the artichokes, use a good-size frying pan with considerable depth. Put the artichokes in the pan, add 6 tablespoons of the olive oil, the bay leaf, and parsley, season with salt and pepper, and pour the lemon soaking water in up to the top of the artichokes, adding more cold water if necessary. Cover the pan and cook over medium-low heat until tender, about 20 minutes. Allow to cool in the frying pan with the remaining liquid.

3. Just before serving, drain the artichoke hearts with great care and place them in a good-size bowl. Add the tomatoes, a few extra drops of lemon juice, and the remaining 2 tablespoons olive oil. Toss well to coat, and serve.

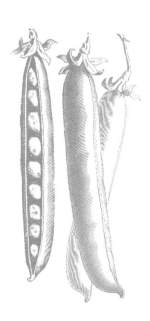

*April*

# Eggs Tonnato

4 hard-boiled eggs, peeled

*Tonnato Sauce*

1 cup mayonnaise, homemade (page 238) or
store-bought

2 tablespoons ketchup

One 3.5-ounce can tuna, drained

1 tablespoons fresh lemon juice

1 shallot, finely chopped

2 tablespoons plain yogurt

1 tablespoon capers, drained and chopped

One 3.5-ounce jar red pimento strips, drained and
thinly sliced, for garnish

Finely chopped fresh dill for garnish

1. Slice the eggs in half lengthwise. Place 2 halves on each of the 4 salad
   plates, cut side up.
2. To make the sauce, in a blender combine the mayonnaise, ketchup, tuna,
   lemon juice, shallot, yogurt, and capers and whirl to blend. Refrigerate
   until ready to use.
3. Just before serving, pour the tuna sauce over the eggs. Decorate the tops
   of the eggs with the pimento strips. Sprinkle some dill over the dish and
   serve.

# Cold Egg, Potato, and Tuna Salad with Mustard-Tarragon Dressing

Makes 6 to 8 servings

## Salad

4 hard-boiled eggs, peeled and coarsely chopped

6 potatoes, peeled, cubed, cooked in boiling salted
water to cover until tender, and drained

1 celery heart, thinly sliced

1 red onion, finely chopped

One 6-ounce can tuna, coarsely chopped

## Tarragon Dressing

One 8-ounce container (1 cup) low-fat sour cream

1 very fresh egg yolk

2 tablespoons fresh lemon juice

1 tablespoon Dijon mustard

2 tablespoons finely chopped fresh tarragon

Salt and freshly ground black pepper to taste

1 head red or green leaf lettuce, separated into
leaves

1. To assemble the salad, put the chopped eggs, potatoes, celery, onion, and tuna in a large salad bowl. Toss gently to combine.

2. Combine all the dressing ingredients in a deep bowl and whisk together until smooth. Check and adjust the seasonings. Pour the dressing over the salad. Toss until well coated with the dressing. Refrigerate until well chilled, at least 2 hours.

3. Arrange the lettuce leaves on a large platter. Spread the salad evenly on top and serve.

*Most people eat
as though they
were fattening
themselves for
the market.*

E. W. Howe

# TARAMASALATA EGG SALAD

*aramasalata is a creamy Greek dip made with carp roe. You may find it in the ethnic food section of your supermarket or in a specialty foods market.*

MAKES 6 SERVINGS

*Salad*

6 hard-boiled eggs, peeled

One 4-ounce jar taramasalata

4 ripe tomatoes, diced

1 medium-size cucumber, peeled, seeded, and diced

1 red or green bell pepper, seeded and diced

1 ripe but firm avocado, peeled, pitted, and diced

1 green apple, peeled, cored, and diced

*Dressing*

6 tablespoons extra virgin olive oil

2 tablespoons fresh lemon juice

1/2 teaspoon Dijon, Meaux, or another French mustard

Salt and freshly ground black pepper to taste

Finely chopped fresh chervil for garnish

1. To make the salad, slice the eggs in half lengthwise. Remove the egg yolks carefully, put them in a small bowl, and mash with a fork. Add the taramasalata and blend together well.

2. Cut a thin slice from the bottom of each egg white so as to allow them to sit flat on a plate. Fill the egg whites with the yolk-taramasalata mixture. Place 2 at the center of each of 6 salad plates.

3. In a large bowl, combine the tomatoes, cucumber, bell pepper, avocado, and apple.

4. In a measuring cup or small bowl, whisk together the dressing ingredients until thickened and pour over the vegetables and fruit in the bowl. Toss well and spoon onto the salad plates around the stuffed eggs. Sprinkle some chervil over the dish and serve.

# SALMON AND CUCUMBER SALAD

*This is an excellent dish to serve as a main course for a simple lunch or brunch.*

MAKES 6 SERVINGS

## Salad

5 pickling cucumbers (like Kirby), cut into thin
   rounds

1 red bell pepper, seeded and cut into bite-size
   pieces

2 cups canned salmon, picked over for skin and
   bones and separated into chunks

1 celery stalk, thinly sliced

1/2 cup crumbled feta cheese

2 scallions, finely chopped

1/4 cup fresh lemon juice

## Dressing

One 8-ounce container (1 cup) low-fat sour cream

2 teaspoons extra virgin olive oil

1 teaspoon Dijon mustard

1 teaspoon honey

Salt and freshly ground black pepper to taste


1 head Boston lettuce, separated into leaves

A few sprigs fresh dill, finely chopped, for garnish

1. In a large bowl, combine all the salad ingredients and mix well.
2. Whisk together the dressing ingredients in a measuring cup or small bowl
   until well combined. Pour over the salad and mix until everything is evenly
   coated. Cover and refrigerate until ready to serve.
3. Just before serving, arrange 3 or 4 lettuce leaves on each of 6 salad plates.
   Place an equal amount of the salad on each plate. Garnish with the dill and
   serve immediately.

*Enough is as good
as a feast.*

John Heywood

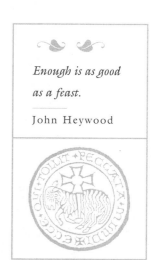

# POTATO SALAD, TUSCAN STYLE

*his is a great salad to serve at a small party. For the best flavor, always serve it at room temperature.*

1 pound potatoes, peeled

2 medium-size or 1 large celery root (celeriac), peeled and cut into matchsticks

2 large carrots, peeled and cut into matchsticks

Juice from 1 lemon

²/₃ cup chopped walnuts

½ cup extra virgin olive oil

Salt and freshly ground black pepper to taste

A few sprigs fresh Italian parsley, finely chopped, for garnish

1. Cook the potatoes in boiling salted water until tender, about 25 minutes. Drain, rinse under cold running water, and allow to cool. Slice them carefully and spread them over a serving platter.
2. Put the celery root and carrots in a large bowl and pour the lemon juice over them. Add the walnuts and mix well. Spread the celery root mixture evenly over the potatoes, leaving the potatoes around the edge of the platter uncovered.
3. Drizzle the olive oil generously over the vegetables, allowing the oil to penetrate in good measure. Season with salt and pepper, sprinkle with the parsley, and serve.

*This is the secret of joy. We shall no longer strive for our own way; but commit ourselves, easily and simply, to God's way, acquiesce in his will and in doing find our peace.*

Evelyn Underhill

# NORTHERN ITALIAN BEAN SALAD

*A*lthough it is traditionally served at room temperature, you can also refrigerate this salad and serve it cold, adding the dressing at the last minute. It is an ideal picnic salad.

MAKES 6 TO 8 SERVINGS

*Salad*

2 cups freshly cooked or canned cannellini beans, drained and rinsed

2 cups freshly cooked or canned chickpeas, drained and rinsed

3 celery stalks, thinly sliced

2 large carrots, peeled and diced

4 scallions (white and light green part), finely chopped

A few sprigs fresh Italian parsley, finely chopped

*Vinaigrette*

1/3 cup extra virgin olive oil

5 tablespoons red wine vinegar

Salt and freshly ground black pepper to taste

1. To make the salad, put the cannellini beans and chickpeas in a large salad bowl. Cook the celery and carrots in boiling salted water for about 5 minutes. Drain, rinse under cold running water, and allow to cool. Add them to the beans along with the scallions and parsley and mix well.

2. Just before serving, whisk the vinaigrette ingredients together in a measuring cup or small bowl until thickened, then pour over the salad. Toss gently, making sure everything is coated evenly. Serve at room temperature.

*April*

# SALADE CROQUANTE

*C*roquant(e) *is a term often used in French to describe the state of vegetables. It means crisp or crunchy (one makes a "crackling" noise when chewing). This is a simple and elegant salad to serve as an appetizer or after a good dinner.*

**MAKES 6 TO 8 SERVINGS**

*Salad*

½ pound mâche or mesclun (mixed salad greens)

½ pound watercress, stems trimmed off

*Vinaigrette*

6 tablespoons fruity hazelnut oil

3 tablespoons tarragon vinegar

1 very fresh egg yolk

1 tablespoon Dijon, Meaux, or another French mustard

Salt and freshly ground black pepper to taste

1. Put the mâche and watercress in a large salad bowl.
2. Put the vinaigrette ingredients in a blender and whirl until the dressing has a thick, uniform consistency. Taste and adjust the seasonings.
3. When ready to serve, pour the vinaigrette over the greens and toss lightly. Serve immediately.

# SALADE AU ROQUEFORT

*This salad, because of its lightness and delicacy, is best served after the main course. It makes an appetizing transition to dessert.*

MAKES 4 TO 6 SERVINGS

*Salad*

1 small head Boston or other butterhead lettuce, separated into leaves

1 small head baby chicory (frisée), separated into leaves

½ pound Roquefort cheese, crumbled

⅔ cup walnut halves

*Vinaigrette*

⅓ cup hazelnut oil

2 tablespoons crème fraîche or heavy cream

3 tablespoons cider vinegar

Salt and freshly ground black pepper to taste

1 bunch fresh chives, finely chopped, for garnish

1. To assemble the salad, toss the lettuce and chicory in a large salad bowl. Add the crumbled cheese and walnuts and toss gently to combine.

2. Combine the vinaigrette ingredients in a blender and whirl for a few seconds until smooth.

3. Just before serving, add the vinaigrette to the salad and toss gently until all the ingredients are well coated. Sprinkle the chopped chives on top and serve.

*French salads are mostly subtle combinations of flavorful small leaves of lettuces and salad greens—no tomatoes thrown in, no chunks of avocado, but oh, those greens!*

Mimi Lubberman

# AVOCADO AND GOAT CHEESE SALAD

*This is a nutritious salad anytime. Present it as a wonderful introduction to a good meal, or serve it as the main course at lunch or brunch.*

MAKES 4 SERVINGS

## Salad

1 head Boston lettuce, separated into leaves

1 large log goat cheese (about $1/2$ pound), cut into
   4 equal slices

2 ripe but firm avocados

## Vinaigrette

6 tablespoons extra virgin olive oil

3 tablespoons fresh lemon juice

Salt and freshly ground black pepper to taste

Leaves from 1 bunch fresh cilantro, finely chopped,
   for garnish

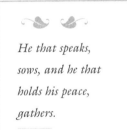

*He that speaks, sows, and he that holds his peace, gathers.*

English proverb

1. Preheat the oven to 350°F or use the broiler instead (no need to preheat). To make the salad, arrange the lettuce leaves on 4 individual salad plates. Place the 4 slices of goat cheese in an ovenproof dish and bake or broil until they begin to melt.

2. While the cheese is in the oven, cut each avocado in half lengthwise, then peel and remove the pit. Place an avocado half, cut side up, atop the lettuce on each plate.

3. In a measuring cup or small bowl, whisk the vinaigrette ingredients together until thickened.

4. When the cheese is done, place a slice in the center of each avocado half. Pour the vinaigrette over each serving and sprinkle with the cilantro. Serve immediately.

# MAY

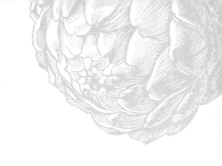

MUSHROOM AND ARUGULA SALAD   80

SPICY POTATO SALAD, COUNTRY STYLE   81

CHILLED CARROT SALAD   82

ROASTED RED PEPPER, CHICORY, AND MOZZARELLA SALAD   83

ASPARAGUS, BEET, AND EGG SALAD   84

EGG, CHEDDAR, AND RICE SALAD   85

SPINACH AND EGG SALAD   86

ITALIAN MIXED SALAD (*INSALATA MISTA*)   87

RADICCHIO AND TOMATO SALAD FROM VENICE
(*INSALATA DI RADICCHIO ROSSO*)   88

ARUGULA AND DANDELION SALAD
WITH ROASTED PEARS   89

LENTIL SALAD, CANTAL STYLE
(*SALADE DE LENTILLES À LA CANTALIENNE*)   90

FARFALLE AND CHICKPEA SALAD   91

PROVENÇAL MESCLUN SALAD
(*SALADE DE MESCLUN À LA PROVENÇALE*)   92

*SALADE DU BARRY*   93

*SALADE RACHEL*   94

ORANGE AND TANGERINE SALAD   95

# MUSHROOM AND ARUGULA SALAD

*This is a light salad that can be served at any time of the year, as a first course, or after the main course.*

**MAKES 4 SERVINGS**

### Salad

½ pound white mushrooms, thinly sliced

1 bunch arugula, stems trimmed off

1 medium-size red onion, finely chopped

### Dressing

6 tablespoons extra virgin olive oil

3 tablespoons fresh lemon juice

1 teaspoon soy sauce

Salt and freshly ground black pepper to taste

A few sprigs fresh chervil or Italian parsley (optional), finely chopped, for garnish

1. To assemble the salad, put the mushrooms, arugula, and onion in a large salad bowl and toss to mix slightly.

2. Just before serving, whisk together the dressing ingredients in a measuring cup or small bowl until thickened. Pour over the salad and toss lightly, making sure everything gets evenly coated. Distribute the salad among 4 salad plates, sprinkle with the chervil, if using, and serve immediately.

# Spicy Potato Salad, Country Style

*This salad is excellent for a family picnic, an informal outdoor party, or any gathering of family and friends.*

MAKES 6 TO 8 SERVINGS

1 pound baby new potatoes, peeled and cut in half

1 cup shelled fresh or frozen peas

1 celery heart, thinly sliced

1 cup Thousand Island Dressing (page 240), prepared ahead of time

1. Cook the potatoes in a large saucepan of boiling salted water until tender but still firm, 15 to 20 minutes. Drain and rinse under cold running water, then drain again thoroughly and place in a large salad bowl.

2. Meanwhile, cook the peas in medium-size saucepan of boiling salted water for 3 minutes. Drain and rinse under cold running water, then drain again and add them to the salad bowl. Add the celery.

3. Pour the dressing over the salad and toss until everything is well coated. Cover and refrigerate for 2 to 3 hours before serving.

*To the quiet mind all things are possible. What is the quiet mind? A quiet mind is one thing which nothing weighs on, nothing worries, which, free from ties and from all self-seeking, is wholly merged into the will of God and dead to its own.*

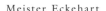

Meister Eckehart

# CHILLED CARROT SALAD

*This salad is an excellent appetizer for lunch or supper. For an attractive presentation, place some lettuce leaves on each plate, then mound the salad on top.*

MAKES 4 TO 6 SERVINGS

7 large carrots, peeled and cut into matchsticks

¼ cup fresh lemon juice

8 fresh mint leaves, finely shredded

1 small onion, diced, or 2 shallots, coarsely chopped

½ cup golden raisins

⅓ cup mayonnaise, homemade (page 238) or store-bought

1 teaspoon Dijon mustard

Salt and freshly ground black pepper to taste

1. Put the carrots in a deep bowl. Add the lemon juice and mix well. Refrigerate for a few hours until ready to serve.

2. Just before serving, remove the bowl from the refrigerator and add the mint, onion, raisins, mayonnaise, and mustard. Season with salt and pepper, and mix together until all the ingredients are well coated with the mayonnaise. Serve immediately, for this salad must be served chilled.

# ROASTED RED PEPPER, CHICORY, AND MOZZARELLA SALAD

*This is an elegant appetizer at any time of the year, but if you prefer, serve it as a main course for lunch or brunch.*

MAKES 6 TO 8 SERVINGS

## Salad

4 large red bell peppers

1 medium-size Vidalia onion, thinly sliced

1/2 pound baby chicory (frisée), stems trimmed off

1 small head radicchio, separated into leaves and cut into strips lengthwise

## Vinaigrette

1/4 cup extra virgin olive oil

3 tablespoons wine vinegar

1 teaspoon Dijon mustard

Salt and freshly ground black pepper to taste

1/2 pound mozzarella cheese, thinly sliced

1. Preheat the oven to 400°F or preheat the broiler. To make the salad, roast or broil the peppers until blackened all over, about 20 minutes, turning them from time to time. When they are done, put them in a paper bag, close it, and allow the peppers to cool. Carefully remove the peppers from the bag, peel off their skins, then wash under cold running water to remove any blackened bits. Pat dry with paper towels. Cut open the peppers and remove the seeds and stem. Slice lengthwise into thin strips. Put the peppers in a deep salad bowl, add the onion, chicory, and radicchio, and toss gently.

2. Just before serving, whisk together the vinaigrette ingredients in a measuring cup or small bowl until thickened, pour over the salad, and toss again until everything is well coated. Serve the salad on individual plates topped with slices of mozzarella.

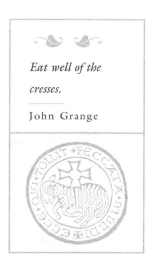

*Eat well of the cresses.*

John Grange

# ASPARAGUS, BEET, AND EGG SALAD

### MAKES 4 SERVINGS

Pinch of salt

20 asparagus stalks, bottoms trimmed off

2 cups peeled and cubed beets

$1/2$ cup extra virgin olive oil

$1/4$ cup cider vinegar

1 tablespoon Dijon, Meaux, or another French
   mustard

1 small shallot, minced

Salt and freshly ground black pepper to taste

1 small head tender escarole, separated into leaves

4 hard-boiled eggs, peeled and chopped

1. Bring a large saucepan full of water to a boil. Add the salt and asparagus and cook for about 3 minutes. Drain and rinse under cold running water, then drain again and set aside.
2. Cook the beets in a medium-size saucepan of boiling salted water until tender, about 6 minutes. Drain and rinse under cold running water, then drain again and set aside.
3. Whisk together the olive oil, vinegar, mustard, shallot, and salt and pepper in a measuring cup or small bowl until thickened.
4. On each of 4 salad plates, arrange 3 escarole leaves. Arrange 5 asparagus on top and place the cubed beets on both sides of the asparagus. Distribute the chopped eggs evenly over each serving. Just before serving, whisk the vinaigrette again, pour evenly over each dish, and serve immediately.

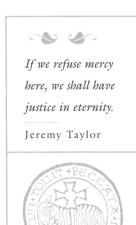

*If we refuse mercy here, we shall have justice in eternity.*

Jeremy Taylor

# EGG, CHEDDAR, AND RICE SALAD

MAKES 8 SERVINGS

4 hard-boiled eggs, peeled and coarsely chopped

2 cups cooked long-grain rice

1 small celery heart, thinly sliced

1 small Vidalia onion, finely chopped

1/2 cup pitted black olives, drained and coarsely chopped

1 cup shelled fresh or frozen peas, cooked in boiling water until tender and drained

One 6-ounce jar pimento strips, drained and coarsely chopped

1 cup diced cheddar cheese

3/4 cup mayonnaise, homemade (page 238) or store-bought

Salt and freshly ground black pepper to taste

1 head leafy lettuce of your choice, separated into leaves

A few parsley sprigs, finely chopped

1. In a large glass salad bowl, combine the eggs, rice, celery, onion, olives, peas, pimentos, and cheese. Toss and mix gently. Add the mayonnaise, season with salt and pepper, and toss until everything is well coated. Cover and refrigerate for at least 2 hours.

2. When ready to serve, arrange the lettuce leaves on a large serving platter. Spoon the egg mixture on the top of the lettuce and spread evenly. Sprinkle the chopped parsley over the top. Serve immediately.

*May*

# SPINACH AND EGG SALAD

*S*erve this salad as an appetizer or after the main course, but always at room temperature.

**MAKES 6 SERVINGS**

*Salad*

**1 pound spinach, trimmed of heavy stems**

**3 hard-boiled eggs, peeled and coarsely chopped**

**12 cherry tomatoes, cut in half**

**1 medium-size red onion, finely chopped**

*Vinaigrette*

**¹/₄ cup extra virgin olive oil**

**5 tablespoons balsamic vinegar**

**1 teaspoon Dijon, Meaux, or another French mustard**

**Salt and freshly ground black pepper to taste**

1. In a large salad bowl, combine all the salad ingredients and toss gently to combine.
2. Whisk together the vinaigrette ingredients in a measuring cup or small bowl until thickened. Pour over the salad, toss to coat everything evenly, and serve immediately.

*Through the Holy Spirit we are restored to paradise, we ascend to the kingdom of heaven, and are reinstated as adopted children. Thanks to the Spirit we obtain the right to call God our Father, we become sharers in the grace of Christ, we are called children of light, and we share in everlasting glory.*

St. Basil the Great

# ITALIAN MIXED SALAD

## (Insalata Mista)

*This salad is usually served after the main course. It is particularly appetizing when the vegetables are in season and, even better, fresh from the garden.*

**MAKES 6 SERVINGS**

### Salad

1 small head Boston or other butterhead lettuce,
  torn into bite-size pieces

4 plum tomatoes, sliced crosswise

1 small cucumber, peeled and cut into thin rounds

1 medium-size carrot, peeled and grated or finely
  shredded

6 radishes, trimmed and thinly sliced

1 small red onion, thinly sliced

### Vinaigrette

1/3 cup extra virgin olive oil

5 tablespoons red wine vinegar

Salt and freshly ground black pepper to taste

1. Put the salad ingredients in a large salad bowl. Toss together lightly.
2. Whisk together the vinaigrette ingredients in a measuring cup or small
   bowl until thickened. Check and adjust the seasonings. Pour over the salad,
   toss to coat everything well, and serve immediately.

# RADICCHIO AND TOMATO SALAD FROM VENICE

## (Insalata di Radicchio Rosso)

*his is an interesting salad that captures the spirit and charm of Venetian cooking. It may be served as an appetizer or after the main course.*

**MAKES 6 SERVINGS**

### Salad

2 small heads radicchio, cut into bite-size pieces

4 ripe tomatoes, sliced

1 medium-size red onion, thinly sliced

1 medium-size red bell pepper, seeded and cut into
   long, thin strips

A few sprigs fresh Italian parsley, finely chopped

### Vinaigrette

⅓ cup extra virgin olive oil

5 tablespoons balsamic vinegar

Salt and freshly ground black pepper to taste

*Beware of the devil, he can hide in a sprig of parsley!*

French proverb

1. Put the salad ingredients in a large salad bowl and toss them together with your hands.
2. Whisk together the vinaigrette ingredients in a measuring cup or small bowl until thickened. Pour over the salad, toss gently to coat everything well, and serve immediately.

# ARUGULA AND DANDELION SALAD
# WITH ROASTED PEARS

*This salad fits the description of a perfect appetizer, but it can also be served after the main course.*

### Salad

3 pears, peeled, cut in half, and cored

$1/2$ pound dandelion greens

7 tablespoons extra virgin olive oil

3 garlic cloves, minced

1 large bunch arugula, stems trimmed off

1 Belgian endive, separated into leaves and cut into
2-inch-long strips

### Vinaigrette

$1/3$ cup extra virgin olive oil

5 tablespoons balsamic vinegar

2 tablespoons honey

Salt and freshly ground black pepper to taste

1. Preheat the oven to 400°F. Put the pear halves in an ovenproof baking dish and roast them for 8 to 10 minutes. Remove them from the oven and allow them to cool.

2. Meanwhile, trim the root ends away from the dandelion greens. Heat the olive oil over medium-low heat in a large skillet, add the garlic, and cook, stirring, for about 30 seconds. Add the dandelion greens and cook, stirring, until wilted, 4 to 5 minutes. Set aside.

3. Put the arugula and endive in a large salad bowl. Add the sautéed greens and roasted pears and toss gently to combine.

4. Whisk together the vinaigrette ingredients in a measuring cup or small bowl until thickened. Just before serving, pour over the salad and toss lightly to coat everything.

*Unquiet meals make ill digestions.*

Shakespeare

# LENTIL SALAD, CANTAL STYLE

## (Salade de Lentilles à la Cantalienne)

antal is part of the Auvergne region in central France, famous for its cultivation of lentils, especially around the town of Puy-de-Dome (hence the name of a certain type of lentil, Le Puy). Serve this salad cold or at room temperature. It is ideal for a picnic because it is easy to transport.

MAKES 4 TO 6 SERVINGS

### Salad

½ pound dried small French lentils (Le Puy lentils are perfect for this recipe)

1 celery heart, thinly sliced

1 medium-size sweet white onion, minced

1 long, thin cucumber, peeled, seeded, and diced

Leaves from 1 small bunch fresh Italian parsley, finely chopped

### Vinaigrette

½ cup extra virgin olive oil

2 tablespoons fresh lemon juice

2 tablespoons red wine vinegar

Salt and freshly ground black pepper to taste

1 head leafy lettuce of your choice, such as Bibb or Boston, separated into leaves

1. To make the salad, cook the lentils in boiling salted water until tender, about 30 minutes. Drain, rinse them under cold running water, and allow them to cool. Put the lentils in a large salad bowl. Add the celery, onion, cucumber, and parsley, toss gently, and place the bowl in the refrigerator until ready to use.

2. Just before serving, whisk together the vinaigrette ingredients in a measuring cup or a small bowl until thickened. Pour over the salad and toss lightly, making sure the vegetables are evenly coated. Arrange a couple of lettuce leaves on each salad plate, mound the lentil mixture on the top, and serve immediately.

# Farfalle and Chickpea Salad

## Salad

¹/₂ pound farfalle (bow tie) pasta

One 15.5-ounce can chickpeas, drained and rinsed

12 ripe cherry tomatoes, cut in half

1 green bell pepper, seeded and finely chopped

1 medium-size Vidalia onion, finely chopped

¹/₂ cup fresh basil leaves, coarsely chopped

¹/₃ cup fresh Italian parsley leaves, finely chopped

1 head Boston or another lettuce of your choice,
  separated into leaves

## Dressing

3 tablespoons plus 1 teaspoon extra virgin olive oil

5 teaspoons Spanish sherry vinegar (preferably
  Jerez) or red wine vinegar

1 garlic clove, minced

Salt and freshly ground black pepper to taste

1. To make the salad, cook the pasta in boiling salted water until *al dente*. Drain and rinse the pasta under cold running water, then drain again, shaking the colander or strainer. Put the pasta in a deep bowl and add the chickpeas, tomatoes, bell pepper, onion, and herbs. Toss well to combine.

2. Place 3 lettuce leaves on each salad plate in the shape of a shamrock.

3. Whisk the dressing ingredients together in a measuring cup or small bowl until thickened. Let stand for 15 minutes before using. (It may be prepared ahead of time.)

4. When ready to serve, pour the dressing into the salad bowl. Toss and blend all the ingredients. Place an equal portion on top of the lettuce on each plate and serve immediately.

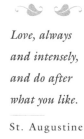

*Love, always
and intensely,
and do after
what you like.*

St. Augustine

# PROVENÇAL MESCLUN SALAD

## (Salade de Mesclun à la Provençale)

1 pound mesclun (mixed salad greens)

1 medium-size red onion, thinly sliced

1/2 cup extra virgin olive oil, plus extra as needed

1/4 cup Raspberry-Scented Vinegar (page 236)

Salt and freshly ground black pepper to taste

6 slices goat cheese or very small logs French chèvre

6 slices French baguette

2 tablespoons dried rosemary

2 tablespoons dried thyme

1. Put the greens in a large salad bowl and add the onion. In a measuring cup or small bowl, whisk together the oil, vinegar, salt, and pepper until thickened. Pour over the greens and toss lightly.

2. Preheat the oven to 350°F or use the broiler instead (no need to preheat). Place a cheese slice on each bread slice. Sprinkle some olive oil on the top of the cheese and crumble some rosemary and thyme over it, pressing the herbs down into the cheese. Place the cheese-topped bread in an ovenproof dish and bake or broil until the cheese bubbles and starts to melt.

3. Divide the greens equally among 6 salad plates. Top each with a slice of the goat cheese–topped bread.

# SALADE DU BARRY

*This salad is ideal any time of the year, but particularly when radishes are in season.*

*Salad*

1 small head cauliflower

24 small radishes, trimmed

1 bunch watercress, stems trimmed off

8 pitted black olives, coarsely chopped

*Vinaigrette*

$1/3$ cup extra virgin olive oil

$1/4$ cup fresh lemon juice

Salt and freshly ground black pepper to taste

1. To make the salad, carefully separate the cauliflower florets from the main stem, making sure they remain intact. Steam them, covered, in the top of a double boiler over simmering water until tender, about 15 minutes, or cook in a large saucepan of boiling salted water, about 5 minutes. Remove them from the heat and rinse under cold running water. Drain and put in a good-size salad bowl or on a platter. Add the radishes, watercress, and olives and toss lightly.

2. Whisk together the vinaigrette ingredients in a measuring cup or small bowl until thickened and pour over the salad. Toss gently until well coated and serve at room temperature.

*Practice the art of aloneness and you will discover the treasury of tranquility. Develop the art of solitude and you will unearth the gift of serenity.*

William A. Ward

# SALADE RACHEL

*This salad is traditionally served cold, which makes it very appropriate for late spring, when aspara-gus is in season, or early summer.*

MAKES 6 SERVINGS

6 medium-size potatoes, peeled and cubed

12 asparagus stalks, bottoms trimmed off and cut into 2-inch lengths

2 shallots, minced

1 celery heart, thinly sliced

One 6-ounce jar artichoke hearts, thoroughly drained and coarsely chopped

$^1/_2$ cup mayonnaise, preferably homemade (page 238)

Salt and freshly ground black pepper to taste

1 hard-boiled egg, peeled and finely chopped, for garnish

1. Cook the potatoes in a large saucepan of boiling salted water just until tender, about 5 minutes. Remove with a slotted spoon and drain, saving the water. Bring that water back to a boil and cook the asparagus in it just until tender, 3 to 4 minutes maximum. Drain and allow both the potatoes and asparagus to cool.

2. Put the potatoes, asparagus, shallots, celery, and artichokes in a large salad bowl and mix together gently. Add the mayonnaise and season with salt and pepper. Mix well and refrigerate until ready to serve.

3. Just before serving, sprinkle the chopped egg over the top of the salad.

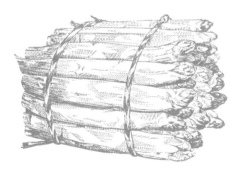

# ORANGE AND TANGERINE SALAD

A fruit salad such as this one needs no salt, sugar, or pepper. The blend of natural flavors suffices.

MAKES 6 TO 8 SERVINGS

### Salad

4 navel oranges, peeled, with white pith removed,
   and separated into segments

4 tangerines, peeled, with white pith removed, and
   separated into segments

1 small red onion, finely chopped

One 1.5-ounce box golden raisins

8 pitted black olives, coarsely chopped

8 fresh mint leaves, chopped

### Dressing

¼ cup extra virgin olive oil

2 tablespoons fresh lemon juice

1. To assemble the salad, put the oranges and tangerines in a large salad bowl. Add the onion, raisins, olives, and mint and toss gently. Refrigerate until ready to serve.

2. Just before serving, drizzle the olive oil and lemon juice over the salad and toss to coat. Serve immediately.

*I read or write, I teach or wonder what is truth,*
*I call upon my God by night and day.*
*I eat and freely drink, I make my rhymes,*
*And snoring sleep, or vigil keep and pray.*
*And very 'war of all my shames I am;*
*O Mary, Christ, have mercy on your man.*

*Apologia pro Vita Sua* (translated by Helen Waddell)

*May*

Habit de Vinaigrié

# JUNE

MUSHROOM AND AVOCADO SALAD    98

EMERALD SALAD, INDONESIAN STYLE    99

GARDEN GREENS AND HERB SALAD    100

ALL-AMERICAN TOSSED SALAD    101

ORZO AND GREEN PEA SALAD    102

VALLE D'AOSTA SALAD (*INSALATA VALLE D'AOSTA*)    103

MOUNT ST.-MICHEL EGG SALAD    104

PESTO-FILLED DEVILED EGGS    105

CATFISH SALAD, GREEK STYLE    106

ITALIAN SALAD WITH COOKED DANDELION GREENS    107

FRESH GREENS AND TUNA SALAD
(*INSALATA CON TONNO*)    108

*SALADE BONNE FEMME*    109

ST. JOHN THE BAPTIST POTATO SALAD    110

STS. PETER AND PAUL SALAD    111

MANGO SALAD PIQUANT    112

# MUSHROOM AND AVOCADO SALAD

*his salad makes an excellent appetizer before any meal. It can also serve as a light luncheon.*

MAKES 4 TO 6 SERVINGS

*Salad*

2 ripe but firm avocados, peeled, pitted, and cubed

1 teaspoon fresh lemon juice

1/2 pound white mushrooms, thinly sliced

1 bunch watercress, stems trimmed off and cut into
  2-inch pieces

1 small bunch fresh chives or scallions, finely
  chopped

3 tablespoons capers, drained

*Dressing*

1/3 cup extra virgin olive oil

3 tablespoons fresh lemon juice

Salt and freshly ground black pepper to taste

1 head Boston lettuce, separated into leaves

1. To assemble the salad, sprinkle the avocado with the lemon juice and put
   in a good-size salad bowl with the other salad ingredients. Toss until well
   combined.
2. Whisk together the dressing ingredients in a measuring cup or small bowl
   until thickened and pour over the salad. Toss lightly to coat everything.
   Place two or three lettuce leaves on each salad plate, arrange the salad on
   top, and serve immediately.

# Emerald Salad, Indonesian Style

## Dressing

⅓ cup hazelnut oil

¼ cup fresh lime or lemon juice

2 teaspoons sugar

1 garlic clove, minced

Pinch of cayenne pepper

Salt to taste

## Salad

1 bunch watercress, stems trimmed off

1 small head Chinese cabbage, leaves trimmed and
   cut into thin strips

3 medium-size carrots, peeled and grated or finely
   shredded

1 medium-size onion, thinly sliced

12 fresh mint leaves, finely shredded

⅓ cup sweetened shredded coconut

1. Combine the dressing ingredients in a blender and whirl at medium speed.
   Let it stand for 1 to 2 hours to allow the garlic flavor to develop.

2. Put the salad ingredients in a large salad bowl, adding the coconut just
   before serving, and mix well.

3. When ready to serve, pour the dressing over the salad and toss lightly, making sure the coconut is well distributed and all elements are evenly coated.
   Serve at room temperature.

*Lettuce, like conversation, requires a good deal of oil, to avoid
friction and keep the company smooth.*

Charles Dudley Warner

# GARDEN GREENS AND HERB SALAD

*This is a light salad to serve after a succulent main course.*

*Salad*

1 small head baby chicory (frisée), stems trimmed off

1 small head Boston lettuce

Small amount of arugula, stems trimmed off

*Vinaigrette*

$1/2$ cup extra virgin olive oil

3 tablespoons sherry vinegar

1 teaspoon fresh lemon juice

1 teaspoon Dijon, Meaux, or another French mustard

Salt and freshly ground black pepper to taste

$1/4$ cup finely chopped fresh cilantro

$1/4$ cup finely chopped fresh chervil

$1/4$ cup finely chopped fresh chives

$1/4$ cup finely chopped fresh Italian parsley

1. Tear the chicory, Boston lettuce, and arugula into bite-size pieces and put in a large salad bowl. Refrigerate until ready to serve.
2. Whisk the vinaigrette ingredients together in a measuring cup or small bowl until thickened. Just before serving, add the herbs to the salad and pour the vinaigrette over it. Toss gently until everything is coated and serve immediately.

*Be praised O my Lord, for Sister Water,*
*For useful is she, lowly, precious and chaste.*

St. Francis of Assisi

# ALL-AMERICAN TOSSED SALAD

**MAKES 6 TO 8 SERVINGS**

## Salad

1 head romaine lettuce, torn into bite-size pieces

1 long, thin cucumber, peeled and sliced

4 medium-size ripe tomatoes, cut into wedges

1 medium-size Spanish or Vidalia onion, thinly sliced

8 radishes, trimmed and thinly sliced

1 green bell pepper, seeded and cut into long, thin strips

## Dressing

½ cup extra virgin olive oil

¼ cup cider vinegar

1 teaspoon Worcestershire sauce

½ teaspoon dry mustard

Salt and freshly ground black pepper to taste

1. Put the salad ingredients in a large salad bowl. If you are preparing the salad ahead of time, cover it with a damp paper towel until ready to serve, and refrigerate if it's going to be several hours. This allows the vegetables to remain fresh and crisp.

2. Just before serving, whisk the dressing ingredients together in a measuring cup or small bowl until thickened. Pour over the salad and toss gently with a large fork and spoon or, if you prefer the French way, with your clean hands. Make sure all the vegetables are evenly coated with dressing. Serve immediately.

# Orzo and Green Pea Salad

MAKES 6 TO 8 SERVINGS

### Salad

2 cups orzo pasta

One 1-pound package frozen peas

1 red bell pepper, seeded and diced

1 red onion, sliced into small pieces

1 celery stalk, thinly sliced

1 garlic clove, minced

1/2 cup pitted black olives, drained and chopped

### Dressing

1/3 cup mayonnaise, homemade (page 238) or store-bought

1 teaspoon Dijon, Meaux, or another French mustard

1 teaspoon fresh lemon juice

Salt and freshly ground black pepper to taste

1. To make the salad, cook the orzo in a large pot of boiling salted water just until tender, 13 or 14 minutes maximum. Drain, rinse under cold running water, and drain again, shaking the colander well. Transfer to a good-size salad bowl.

2. While the pasta is cooking, cook the frozen peas in boiling salted water in a separate saucepan until tender; do not overcook. Drain and add to the orzo in the salad bowl. Add the remaining salad ingredients.

3. Whisk the dressing ingredients together in a measuring cup or small bowl until smooth. Pour over the salad and mix until well coated. Refrigerate for at least 3 hours before serving. Serve cold.

*Twelve Months of Monastery Salads*

# VALLE D'AOSTA SALAD

## *(Insalata Valle d'Aosta)*

*his is an excellent salad for a picnic or outdoor lunch or supper. If you are taking it to a picnic, the vinaigrette should be packed in a small, tightly covered container and added to the salad at the last minute.*

**MAKES 4 TO 6 SERVINGS**

### *Vinaigrette*

⅓ cup extra virgin olive oil

6 tablespoons balsamic vinegar or red wine vinegar

1 garlic clove, minced

Salt and freshly ground black pepper to taste

### *Salad*

2 fennel bulbs, stalks discarded and bulbs thinly sliced

1 bunch radishes, trimmed and thinly sliced

2 cups diced Gruyère or other cheese of your choice

½ cup pitted black olives, drained and sliced

2 scallions (white and light green parts), thinly sliced

1. Prepare the vinaigrette at least 1 hour ahead of time to let the garlic flavor develop. Whisk the ingredients together in a measuring cup or small bowl until thickened.
2. Combine the salad ingredients in a deep salad bowl and toss gently.
3. Just before serving pour the vinaigrette over the salad and toss lightly until everything is well coated. Serve immediately.

*God is always opening His hand to give.*

Spanish proverb

# MOUNT ST.-MICHEL EGG SALAD

*Serve this salad on individual plates or, if you prefer, arrange it on a large platter so each diner may help himself or herself.*

MAKES 4 SERVINGS

## Salad

4 medium-size ripe tomatoes, sliced

4 hard-boiled eggs, peeled and sliced

2 small cucumbers, peeled and cut into thin rounds

16 Kalamata olives, pitted

Leaves from 1 small bunch fresh basil, finely
chopped

## Dressing

1/2 cup plus 2 tablespoons extra virgin olive oil

3 tablespoons fresh lemon juice

Salt and freshly ground black pepper to taste

1. To assemble the salad, place 4 salad plates on the table. On each plate
   arrange the slices of 1 of the tomatoes, the slices of 1 of the eggs, and of
   1/2 cucumber. Place 4 olives on each plate. Sprinkle some of the basil over
   each plate.

2. Whisk the dressing ingredients together in a measuring cup or small bowl
   until thickened and pour equally over each portion. Serve immediately.

*Blessed is he who has found his work; let him ask no other blessedness.*
*He has a work, a life-purpose; he has found it, and will follow it!*
*Labor is life: from the inmost heart of the worker rises his God-given*
*force, the sacred, celestial life-essence breathed into him by Almighty God.*

Thomas Carlyle

# PESTO-FILLED DEVILED EGGS

6 hard-boiled eggs, peeled

¼ cup extra virgin olive oil, plus more for drizzling

2 garlic cloves, peeled

8 leaves fresh basil

Salt and freshly ground black pepper to taste

6 medium-size ripe tomatoes, sliced

1 small red onion, finely chopped

Leaves from 1 small bunch fresh basil, finely chopped, for garnish

24 Kalamata olives, pitted

1. Slice the eggs lengthwise in half. Carefully remove the egg yolks and place them in a bowl. Mash them with a fork.

2. Place the olive oil, garlic, and basil leaves in a blender and whirl until ground and smooth. Season with salt and pepper and whirl again to incorporate. Add this pesto to the mashed egg yolks and mix well. Fill the egg whites with the pesto mixture.

3. Place 2 stuffed egg halves on each of 6 serving plates. Next to the eggs, place the slices from 1 tomato. Sprinkle some finely chopped onion and chopped basil on top of the tomatoes. Place 4 olives on each plate. Drizzle some olive oil on top of the tomatoes. Sprinkle on some salt and pepper to taste. Serve immediately.

# CATFISH SALAD, GREEK STYLE

*This is an excellent hot weather salad. Served for lunch, it is a whole meal in itself.*

MAKES 6 TO 8 SERVINGS

### Salad

2 cups water

1/2 pound catfish fillets

1 tablespoon fresh lemon juice

1 pound spinach, trimmed of heavy stems and torn into bite-size pieces

1 medium-size red onion, finely chopped

1 cup Kalamata olives, drained, pitted, and cut in half

18 cherry tomatoes,

1/2 pound feta cheese, crumbled

### Greek Vinaigrette

1/2 cup extra virgin olive oil, preferably Greek

1/4 cup fresh lemon juice

2 tablespoons white wine vinegar

1 garlic clove, minced

1 tablespoon chopped fresh oregano

1 tablespoon chopped fresh basil

1 tablespoon chopped fresh thyme

Salt and freshly ground black pepper to taste

*There is no love sincerer than the love of food.*

George Bernard Shaw

1. To make the salad, bring the water to a boil in a large skillet. Add the catfish and lemon juice, cover, reduce the heat to medium, and cook just until you can flake the fish with a fork, about 10 minutes. Remove the fish from the water and allow it to cool. Cut into small pieces, put in a bowl, cover, and chill for at least 1 hour in the refrigerator.

2. Put the spinach in a large salad bowl, then add the onion, olives, tomatoes, feta, and catfish. Toss gently to combine.

3. Whisk the vinaigrette ingredients together in a measuring cup or small bowl until thickened. Pour over the salad and toss gently until everything is evenly coated. Serve immediately.

# ITALIAN SALAD WITH COOKED DANDELION GREENS

*Serve this delicious salad as an appetizer at the beginning of a special meal. Because the dandelions are cooked, you can use older leaves in this recipe.*

MAKES 6 SERVINGS

## Salad

¼ cup extra virgin olive oil

3 garlic cloves, minced

½ pound dandelion greens, stems trimmed off

1 small head radicchio, shredded

1 small head baby chicory (frisée), separated into
   leaves and cut in half

1 medium-size red onion, thinly sliced

3 strips bacon (optional), fried until crisp, drained,
   and crumbled into ½-inch pieces

## Vinaigrette

6 tablespoons extra virgin olive oil

3 tablespoons balsamic vinegar

1 tablespoon orange juice

Salt and freshly ground black pepper to taste

1. To make the salad, heat the olive oil in a large skillet over medium-low heat, add the garlic, and cook, stirring, for about 30 seconds. Add the dandelion greens and cook, stirring, for 3 to 4 minutes, until wilted. Remove from the heat.

2. Put the radicchio, chicory, and onion in a good-size salad bowl. Add the cooked dandelion greens and bacon, if using. Toss to mix the salad.

3. Whisk the vinaigrette ingredients together in a measuring cup or small bowl until thickened. At the last minute, pour over the salad and toss lightly, making sure all the ingredients are evenly coated. Serve immediately.

*If you are hungry, can't you be content with the wholesome roots of the earth?*

Richard Sheridan

# FRESH GREENS AND TUNA SALAD
## (Insalata con Tonno)

*easy to prepare, this salad combines the sedative flavor of greens with the refreshing taste of the sea. It is an all-year-round salad, but is most appropriate during the summer and early autumn.*

**MAKES 6 SERVINGS**

*Salad*

½ pound baby spinach

1 small bunch arugula or watercress, stems trimmed
   off

1 small head baby chicory (frisée), leaves separated
   and cut in half

1 medium-size red onion, thinly sliced

Two 6-ounce cans tuna, drained and coarsely
   chopped

*Vinaigrette*

⅓ cup extra virgin olive oil

5 tablespoons red wine vinegar

Salt and freshly ground black pepper to taste

1. To assemble the salad, put the greens in a large salad bowl, add the onion
   and tuna, and mix well.
2. Whisk the vinaigrette ingredients together in a measuring cup or small
   bowl until thickened and pour over the salad. Toss well to coat evenly and
   serve immediately.

*Be silent about great things; let them grow inside you.*
*Never discuss them; discussion is so limiting and distracting.*
*It makes things grow smaller.*

Friedrich von Hugel

# SALADE BONNE FEMME

*B*onne femme *is a common expression in France and means "good woman"; in this case,* Salade Bonne Femme *loosely translates as "a salad from the lady of the house." It is equally appetizing during the winter or in the summer months, when the string beans are in season.*

MAKES 6 TO 8 SERVINGS

*Salad*

½ pound white mushrooms

2 tablespoons fresh lemon juice

½ pound very thin French string beans *(haricots verts)*, ends trimmed off

3 shallots, minced

*Vinaigrette*

6 tablespoons extra virgin olive oil

3 tablespoons tarragon vinegar

Salt and freshly ground black pepper to taste

1 hard-boiled egg, peeled and finely chopped, for garnish

1. To make the salad, thinly slice the mushrooms, place them in a large salad bowl, and sprinkle the lemon juice over them. Toss lightly and set them aside.

2. Cook the string beans in boiling salted water until tender, about 5 minutes. Do not overcook them. Drain, then rinse under cold running water and drain again, shaking the colander or strainer until all the water is gone. Add the beans to the salad bowl, add the shallots, and toss the salad lightly.

3. Whisk the vinaigrette ingredients together in a measuring cup or small bowl until thickened. Just before serving, pour over the salad, toss until coated, and sprinkle the chopped egg over the top.

# St. John the Baptist Potato Salad

*St. John the Baptist is also called "the Precursor," for he was given the task of preparing the way for the preaching of Christ. Since he is a desert saint, he is a special model for monks, the prototype of monks. (Monastic life started in the desert.) His solemnity is celebrated on June 24. This salad may be served as a side dish to a meat or fish entrée.*

### MAKES 6 TO 8 SERVINGS

## Salad

1 pound new potatoes, peeled

One 15.5-ounce can chickpeas, drained and rinsed

3 shallots, finely chopped

12 pitted green olives, coarsely chopped

## Dressing

$1/3$ cup extra virgin olive oil

3 tablespoons Spanish sherry vinegar (preferably Jerez)

1 teaspoon fresh lemon juice

1 garlic clove, minced

Salt and freshly ground black pepper to taste

$1/3$ cup chopped fresh Italian parsley for garnish

*For everything that lives is holy, life delights in life.*

William Blake

1. To make the salad, cook the potatoes in boiling salted water until just cooked through; start checking at about 15 minutes. (Test with a fork.) Drain and allow to cool, then dice. Put the potatoes in a large salad bowl. Add the chickpeas, shallots, and olives and mix well. Refrigerate the salad until ready to serve.

2. One hour before serving, whisk the dressing ingredients in a measuring cup or small bowl until thickened. Let it stand for 1 hour to let the garlic flavor develop.

3. When ready to serve, pour the vinaigrette over the salad and toss to coat. Sprinkle the parsley over the top and serve.

# STS. PETER AND PAUL SALAD

*Sts. Peter and Paul, great apostles of the Lord, both suffered martyrdom in Rome and thus they are celebrated together in the liturgy on June 29. This salad is always served as an appetizer.*

MAKES 6 TO 8 SERVINGS

*Salad*

12 Boston lettuce leaves

1 cup fresh bean sprouts, rinsed with boiling water and patted dry

4 plum tomatoes, cut into thin wedges

1 large red bell pepper, seeded and cut into long, thin strips

1 green bell pepper, seeded and cut into long, thin strips

2 celery stalks, thinly sliced

1 fennel bulb, stalks discarded and bulb thinly sliced

3 tablespoons sesame seeds (optional), toasted in a dry skillet over medium heat until lightly browned

*Dressing*

1/3 cup extra virgin olive oil

1/4 cup soy sauce

1/3 cup white wine vinegar or distilled vinegar

1/2 teaspoon fresh lemon juice

1/2 teaspoon ground ginger or peeled and grated fresh ginger

1 teaspoon sugar

Salt and white pepper to taste

2 hard-boiled eggs, peeled and coarsely chopped, for garnish

1. To assemble the salad, place 2 lettuce leaves on each salad plate in a decorative fashion. In a large salad bowl, combine the bean sprouts, tomatoes, peppers, celery, fennel, and sesame seeds, if using. Mix gently.
2. Combine the dressing ingredients in a blender and whirl for a few seconds to mix well. Pour over the salad and toss to coat. Divide the salad evenly among the plates, sprinkle with the chopped eggs, and serve immediately.

# Mango Salad Piquant

*This salad should always be served as an appetizer. It is particularly appealing during the summer months.*

**MAKES 6 SERVINGS**

### Salad

2 large ripe mangoes, peeled and flesh cut off the pit and into cubes

2 medium-size Belgian endives, separated into leaves and thinly sliced

1 medium-size red onion, minced

1 red bell pepper, seeded and cut into long, thin strips

1 green bell pepper, seeded and cut into long, thin strips

### Dressing

$1/3$ cup extra virgin olive oil

3 tablespoons fresh lemon juice

$1/2$ teaspoon ground ginger

Pinch of cayenne pepper

Salt and freshly ground black pepper to taste

1 head leafy lettuce of your choice

A few sprigs fresh cilantro, finely chopped, for garnish

*The grave of one who dies for the truth is holy ground.*

German proverb

1. Combine all the salad ingredients in a good-size salad bowl.
2. Whisk together the dressing ingredients in a measuring cup or small bowl until thickened. Taste and adjust the seasonings, then pour it over the salad and toss gently until everything is evenly coated. Refrigerate for 1 hour.
3. Just before serving, place a few lettuce leaves on each salad plate. Place the salad mixture in the center, making sure all the ingredients are equally distributed. Garnish with the cilantro and serve immediately.

# JULY

RUSSIAN POTATO SALAD    114

MIDDLE EASTERN TABBOULEH SALAD    115

TOMATO SALAD, ALSATIAN STYLE *(TOMATES À L'ALSACIENNE)*    116

COSTA BRAVA EGG-AND-TUNA-FILLED TOMATOES    117

MINT-FLAVORED FUSILLI SALAD    118

MACARONI SALAD    119

TOMATO AND OLIVE SALAD FROM THE LAZIO *(INSALATA DI POMODORI E OLIVE NERE)*    120

SICILIAN BEAN AND POTATO SALAD *(INSALATA ALLA CONTADINA)*    121

ITALIAN SUMMER SALAD *(INSALATA D'ESTATE)*    122

TUSCAN SALAD *(PANZANELLA)*    123

*SALADE CAMILLE*    124

ZUCCHINI SALAD, BASQUE STYLE *(SALADE DES COURGETTES À LA BASQUAISE)*    125

ST. BENEDICT SALAD    126

PROPHET ELIJAH LENTIL SALAD    127

ST. MARY MAGDALENE SALAD    128

ST. JOAQUIM SALAD    129

ST. ANNE SALAD    130

STUFFED MELON SALAD    131

SUMMER FRUIT PLATTER    132

# RUSSIAN POTATO SALAD

6 large potatoes, peeled and cubed

2 large carrots, peeled and cubed

2 medium-size beets, peeled and cubed

1 cup frozen peas

3 gherkins or cornichons, thinly sliced

$^1/_2$ cup pitted green olives, drained and chopped

3 hard-boiled eggs, peeled and chopped

1 medium-size onion, finely chopped

$^1/_2$ cup mayonnaise, homemade (page 238) or store-bought

2 teaspoons Dijon, Meaux, or another French mustard

Minced fresh dill (optional) for garnish

1. Cook separately in boiling salted water the potatoes (about 4 to 5 minutes), carrots (about 5 minutes), beets (about 5 minutes), and peas (about 3 minutes) until each is just tender. Drain and rinse under cold running water and refrigerate until cold.

2. Put the chilled vegetables in a deep salad bowl. Add the gherkins, olives, eggs, and onion and toss gently to combine well.

3. Mix the mayonnaise and mustard together well in small bowl or measuring cup. Pour over the salad and toss again until everything is evenly coated. Cover and chill for several hours before serving.

4. When ready to serve, garnish the top of the salad with the dill.

# Middle Eastern Tabbouleh Salad

Makes 4 to 6 servings

1½ cups bulgur

3 cups cold water

Pinch of salt

12 cherry tomatoes, cut in half

2 medium-size green bell peppers, seeded and diced

1 medium-size cucumber, peeled, quartered lengthwise, seeded, and diced

A few sprigs fresh Italian parsley, finely chopped

14 fresh mint leaves, finely shredded

3 shallots, minced

2 small garlic cloves, minced

⅓ cup extra virgin olive oil

¼ cup fresh lemon juice

Freshly ground black pepper to taste

1. In a medium-size bowl, soak the bulgur in cold water to cover for about 30 minutes. Drain and transfer to a good-size saucepan. Add the 3 cups of water and the salt and bring to a rapid boil. Cover, reduce the heat to medium-low, and continue to cook until the bulgur absorbs all the liquid, about 30 minutes. Rinse it under cold running water and drain thoroughly. Transfer to a large salad bowl.

2. Add the tomatoes, peppers, cucumber, parsley, mint, shallots, and garlic to the salad bowl and toss lightly to combine. Refrigerate at least 1 hour, or until ready to serve.

3. Just before serving, add the olive oil and lemon juice, season with salt and pepper, and toss everything to coat well. Serve immediately.

*The fullest possible enjoyment in this life is to be found by reducing our ego to zero.*

G. K. Chesterton

# TOMATO SALAD, ALSATIAN STYLE

## (*Tomates à l'Alsacienne*)

*This is an enticing salad to serve during the summer months or in early fall, when tomatoes are at their very best. I highly recommend it as a simple main-course lunch.*

**MAKES 6 SERVINGS**

### *Salad*

6 plum tomatoes

6 small red potatoes, cooked in boiling salted water
    just until tender, drained, peeled, and quartered

1 medium-size red onion, finely chopped

$\frac{1}{2}$ cup fresh chervil leaves, finely chopped

### *Vinaigrette*

1 teaspoon Dijon mustard

$\frac{1}{2}$ cup extra virgin olive oil

$\frac{1}{4}$ cup tarragon vinegar

Salt and freshly ground black pepper to taste


6 hard-boiled eggs, peeled and quartered

Coarsely chopped pitted green olives for garnish

1. To assemble the salad, put the tomatoes and potatoes in a deep bowl and sprinkle with the onion and chervil.

2. Whisk together the vinaigrette ingredients in a measuring cup or small bowl until thickened. Pour over the salad and toss gently a few times. Distribute the salad evenly among 6 plates. Arrange 4 egg quarters attractively on each plate, then sprinkle some of the olives over the top and serve immediately.

*It is next to impossible to give absolute directions for the compounding of a salad, so far as the precise amount of each component is concerned.*

George H. Ellwanger

# COSTA BRAVA
# EGG-AND-TUNA-FILLED TOMATOES

MAKES 8 SERVINGS

One 6-ounce can tuna, drained

1 small celery heart, thinly sliced

1 medium-size cucumber, peeled, seeded, and diced

1 medium-size red onion, finely chopped

3 hard-boiled eggs, peeled and coarsely chopped

10 pitted green olives, coarsely chopped

1/2 cup mayonnaise, homemade (page 238) or store-bought, or more to taste

A few sprigs fresh dill, finely chopped

Salt and freshly ground black pepper to taste

8 medium-size ripe tomatoes

1 head leafy lettuce of your choice, separated into leaves

1. Put the tuna in a deep bowl and flake it with a fork. Add the celery, cucumber, onion, eggs, and olives and mix well. Add the mayonnaise and dill and season with salt and pepper. Mix well to blend all the ingredients. Refrigerate for at least 3 hours, or until ready to serve.

2. About 1 hour before you are ready to serve, core the tomatoes, then cut them into perfect halves and scoop out their insides, taking care not to puncture the skins. Turn them upside down to get rid of all the water. Fill the tomato cavities with the egg-and-tuna mixture, heaping it a bit high. Place 3 lettuce leaves in the form of a shamrock on each of 8 salad plates. Place 2 tomato halves in the center. Serve immediately.

*The life of the soul is truth and the awareness of the soul is love.*

St. Bernard of Clairvaux

# MINT-FLAVORED FUSILLI SALAD

MAKES 6 TO 8 SERVINGS

## Salad

1 pound fusilli pasta

6 plum tomatoes, quartered

1 medium-size cucumber, peeled, quartered
   lengthwise, seeded, and cut into small chunks

1 medium-size Vidalia onion, thinly sliced

1 fennel bulb, stalks discarded and bulb thinly
   sliced

1/3 cup coarsely chopped fresh mint

## Dressing

6 tablespoons extra virgin olive oil

4 teaspoons fresh lemon juice

1/2 teaspoon dry mustard

Salt and freshly ground black pepper to taste

1. To make the salad, cook the fusilli in boiling salted water. They must remain *al dente*. Drain and rinse under cold running water. Drain again, shaking the colander. Put the fusilli in a large salad bowl and add the remaining salad ingredients.

2. Whisk together the dressing ingredients in a measuring cup or small bowl until thickened. Pour over the salad and toss to coat well. Serve the salad at room temperature or refrigerate for 30 minutes and serve cool.

# MACARONI SALAD

## Salad

1 pound macaroni

4 hard-boiled eggs, peeled and coarsely chopped

3 celery stalks, thinly sliced

4 gherkins or cornichons, thinly sliced

$1/2$ cup pitted green olives, drained and coarsely chopped

1 small red onion, finely chopped

## Dressing

$1/2$ cup mayonnaise, homemade (page 238) or store-bought

1 tablespoon Dijon, Meaux, or another mustard of your choice

$1/4$ cup finely chopped fresh dill

Freshly ground black pepper to taste

1. To make the salad, cook the macaroni in boiling salted water until *al dente*. Drain and rinse under cold running water. Drain again, shaking the colander. Put the macaroni in a large bowl and add the remaining salad ingredients.

2. Whisk the dressing ingredients together in a measuring cup or small bowl until smooth. Pour over the salad and blend well, making sure all the ingredients are equally coated. Cover and refrigerate for several hours; serve cold.

*The weakest among us has a gift, however seemingly trivial, which is peculiar to him and which worthily used will be a gift also to his race.*

John Ruskin

# TOMATO AND OLIVE SALAD
# FROM THE LAZIO
## *(Insalata di Pomodori e Olive Nere)*

his is a salad of subtle contrasts and makes a glorious appetizer during the months when tomatoes are in season. The vinaigrette consists mostly of olive oil, which should be of superior quality; the touch of vinegar is there to accentuate the flavors.

**MAKES 6 SERVINGS**

*Salad*

6 large ripe tomatoes, thickly sliced

1 medium-size red onion, thinly sliced

12 slices fresh mozzarella cheese

30 pitted black olives

12 fresh basil leaves, finely shredded

*Vinaigrette*

$1/3$ cup extra virgin olive oil, or more if needed

2 tablespoons red wine vinegar

Salt and freshly ground black pepper to taste

*Eat bread at*
*pleasure,*
*Drink wine by*
*measure.*

English proverb

1. To assemble the salad, arrange the tomato slices attractively on 6 salad plates. Arrange the onion on the top of the tomatoes. Place 2 mozzarella slices on the top of each serving. Place 5 olives on each plate. Garnish the top with the shredded basil.

2. Whisk together the vinaigrette ingredients in a measuring cup or small bowl until well mixed. Sprinkle evenly over each plate and serve immediately.

# SICILIAN BEAN AND POTATO SALAD
## *(Insalata alla Contadina)*

*his salad may be served slightly cold or at room temperature. It is an excellent summer salad, ideal for a picnic or a party.*

MAKES 6 TO 8 SERVINGS

*Vinaigrette*

1/2 cup extra virgin olive oil

5 tablespoons red wine vinegar

1 garlic clove, minced

Salt and freshly ground black pepper to taste

*Salad*

1 pound new red potatoes, cooked in boiling water
   until just tender, drained, peeled, and quartered

1/2 pound green string beans, ends trimmed off,
   cooked in boiling water until crisp-tender,
   drained, and cut into 2-inch lengths

1/2 pound yellow (wax) string beans, ends trimmed
   off, cooked in boiling water until crisp-tender,
   drained, and cut into 2-inch lengths

1 red onion, coarsely chopped

1/2 cup pitted black olives, drained and chopped

3 tablespoons capers, drained

4 small gherkins or cornichons, thinly sliced

1. A few hours before serving, whisk together the vinaigrette ingredients in a measuring cup or small bowl until thickened, and let stand to allow the garlic flavor to develop.
2. Combine all the salad ingredients in a large serving bowl and refrigerate for at least 2 hours.
3. Just before serving, whisk the vinaigrette again, pour over the salad, and toss gently until everything is well coated.

# ITALIAN SUMMER SALAD
## (Insalata d'Estate)

*This is a perfect summer salad to serve after a succulent main course. In the Italian tradition, this sort of salad restores and cleanses one's system.*

MAKES 6 TO 8 SERVINGS

*Salad*

1 medium-size head romaine lettuce, torn into bite-size pieces

1 small head baby chicory (frisée), torn into bite-size pieces

4 medium-size firm ripe tomatoes, sliced

1 medium-size cucumber, cut into thin rounds (if not fresh from the garden, you'll want to peel it)

1 medium-size Vidalia onion or red onion, thinly sliced

10 fresh basil leaves, finely shredded

*Vinaigrette*

$1/3$ cup extra virgin olive oil

$1/4$ cup red wine vinegar

Salt and freshly ground black pepper to taste

1. Combine the salad ingredients in a large salad bowl and toss to mix well.
2. Just before serving, whisk the vinaigrette ingredients together in a measuring cup or small bowl until thickened. Pour over the salad, toss well to coat, and serve immediately.

*The greatest thing a man can do for his Heavenly Father is to be kind to some of His other children.*

Henry Drummond

# Tuscan Salad

## (*Panzanella*)

*This particular salad is very popular in Italian monasteries, where the monks often put to use day-old bread in the preparation of soups or salads. In a monastery, where both frugality and simplicity are essential, nothing gets wasted and monks are rather clever at finding a good use for almost anything.*

MAKES 6 TO 8 SERVINGS

### Salad

5 cups cubed stale country bread with the crust

8 pounds ripe plum tomatoes, cored and cubed

1 red onion, finely chopped

1 medium-size cucumber, peeled, seeded, and diced

8 pitted black olives, chopped

6 pitted green olives, chopped

1/2 cup packed fresh basil leaves, cut into thin strips

1 tablespoon fresh thyme leaves or 1 teaspoon dried thyme

### Vinaigrette

6 tablespoons extra virgin olive oil

3 tablespoons red wine vinegar

Salt and freshly ground black pepper to taste

1. To assemble the salad, put the bread, tomatoes, onion, cucumber, and olives in a good-size salad bowl. Add the basil and thyme.

2. Whisk together the vinaigrette ingredients in a measuring cup or small bowl until thickened. Pour slowly over the salad and toss gently to coat everything. Set the salad aside, but not in the refrigerator, for about 30 minutes, until the bread cubes soften. Just before serving, check the seasonings and adjust accordingly. This salad should be kept and served at room temperature.

# SALADE CAMILLE

his salad is often served as an appetizer, but it can also be the main course for a summer lunch.

MAKES 6 SERVINGS

*Salad*

6 medium-size ripe tomatoes, sliced

3 small ripe but firm avocados

2 tablespoons fresh lemon juice

Two 6-ounce cans tuna, drained and coarsely chopped

3 hard-boiled eggs, peeled and quartered lengthwise

12 pitted black olives

*Vinaigrette*

$1/3$ cup hazelnut oil or extra virgin olive oil

$1/4$ cup red wine vinegar

1 tablespoon Dijon, Meaux, or another French mustard

1 shallot, minced

Salt and freshly ground black pepper to taste

A few sprigs fresh Italian parsley, finely chopped, for garnish

1. To assemble the salad, choose an attractive, good-size platter to present and serve this dish. Place the tomatoes slices in a circle around the outer edge. Cut the avocados in half, remove the peel and pits, and carefully dice. Transfer the dice to a small bowl, pour the lemon juice over them, and mix gently. Place the diced avocado in the center of the platter between the tomato slices. Arrange the chopped tuna over the avocado and place the egg slices between the tomato slices. Place the olives on the outer edge of the salad around the tomatoes.

2. Put the vinaigrette ingredients in a blender and whirl for a few seconds. Pour evenly over every part of the salad. Sprinkle the top with the parsley and serve immediately.

# ZUCCHINI SALAD, BASQUE STYLE

## (Salade des Courgettes à la Basquaise)

*This salad makes an interesting appetizer for an outdoor summer meal. It is also an attractive dish to present at an informal party.*

MAKES 6 TO 8 SERVINGS

*Salad*

4 medium-size very fresh zucchini, cubed

6 plum tomatoes, coarsely chopped

1 medium-size red or white onion, coarsely chopped

1 red or yellow bell pepper, seeded and diced

*Vinaigrette*

½ cup extra virgin olive oil

¼ cup red wine vinegar

Salt and freshly ground black pepper to taste

Leaves from 1 small bunch fresh Italian parsley,
finely chopped, for garnish

1. To make the salad, cook the zucchini in boiling salted water for 2 to 3 minutes maximum, so it remains crisp. Drain, then rinse under cold running water. Drain again, shaking the colander or strainer well, and put the zucchini in a good-size salad bowl. Add the tomatoes, onion, and bell peppers and toss gently to combine.

2. Just before serving, whisk the vinaigrette ingredients together in a measuring cup or small bowl until thickened. Pour over the salad and toss lightly until the ingredients are evenly coated. Sprinkle with the parsley and serve immediately.

*God is a husbandman, His seed His only Word,*
*The ploughshare is His Spirit, my heart the sowing ground.*

Angelus Silesius

# St. Benedict Salad

*St. Benedict is the father and patriarch of Western monks. He was born in Norcia, Italy, around* A.D. *480 and died in Monte Cassino circa 547. His monastic rule, followed by countless monks and nuns throughout the centuries, was very influential in shaping Western civilization and the history of Europe. St. Benedict is the patron saint of Europe. His feast day is celebrated on July 11.*

### Makes 6 servings

*Salad*

1½ cups rice

3 medium-size cucumbers, peeled

½ cup golden raisins

½ cup pitted black olives, drained and coarsely chopped

1 tablespoon capers, drained

2 shallots, finely chopped

2 tablespoons finely chopped fresh mint

2 tablespoons fresh lemon juice

*Curry Mayonnaise*

½ cup mayonnaise, homemade (page 238) or store-bought

1 garlic clove, minced

1 teaspoon curry powder

Lettuce leaves

1. To make the salad, cook the rice in salted water according to the package directions but remove from the heat when cooked but still firm. Drain any leftover water and then rinse under cold running water. Allow the rice to cool, and put it in a large salad bowl.

2. While the rice is cooling, cut the cucumbers in half lengthwise and scoop out the seeds. Cut into cubes and let stand for about 30 minutes. Add them to the rice in the bowl. Add the raisins, olives, capers, shallots, mint, and lemon juice and mix well.

3. Whisk the dressing ingredients together in a measuring cup or small bowl until smooth. Pour over the salad and toss to coat. Chill the salad for several hours before serving. Serve cold, mounded on top of a few lettuce leaves.

# PROPHET ELIJAH LENTIL SALAD

*This is a terrific salad for a picnic or for dining outside on a summer evening, especially around July 20, the Feast of St. Elias, who was referred to in the Old Testament as the prophet Elijah.*

**MAKES 6 TO 8 SERVINGS**

## *Salad*

1 pound dried black or green French lentils, picked over and rinsed

6 cups water

Pinch of salt

1 celery heart, finely chopped

1 fennel bulb, stalks discarded and bulb finely chopped

1 red onion, finely chopped

2 small pickling cucumbers (like Kirby), cut into small pieces

Leaves from 1 bunch fresh cilantro, finely chopped

A few sprigs fresh Italian parsley, finely chopped

## *French Deluxe Dressing*

1/3 cup extra virgin olive oil

1/4 cup fresh lemon juice

1 tablespoon prepared chili sauce

1 tablespoon Dijon or other mustard of your choice

1 teaspoon prepared horseradish

1 garlic clove, minced

1/2 teaspoon paprika

Salt and freshly ground black pepper to taste

1. To make the salad, put the lentils, water, and salt in a large saucepan and bring to a boil. Reduce the heat to medium and simmer for 15 minutes. (It is important that the lentils not be overcooked, but remain firm and crunchy.) Drain, rinse under cold running water, shake the colander or strainer well, and put the lentils in a large salad bowl. Add the celery, fennel, onion, and cucumber and toss gently to combine. Add the cilantro and parsley and toss a few more times.
2. Combine the dressing ingredients in a blender and whirl until smooth. Pour over the salad and mix until everything is well coated. Cover and chill in the refrigerator for at least 2 or 3 hours before serving. Serve cold.

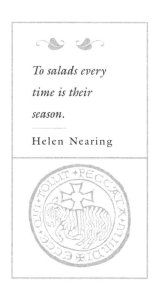

*To salads every time is their season.*

Helen Nearing

# ST. MARY MAGDALENE SALAD

*St. Mary Magdalene is the woman whom Jesus healed of "seven devils." She was also the first witness to the resurrection of Christ. Her feast is kept on July 22.*

**MAKES 4 SERVINGS**

### Salad

1 bunch arugula

1 bunch mâche

1 medium-size red onion, thinly sliced

1 small log goat cheese (about ¼ pound)

### Vinaigrette

6 tablespoons extra virgin olive oil

2 tablespoons red or white wine vinegar

1 teaspoon salt

½ teaspoon freshly ground black pepper

1. Preheat the oven to 350°F. To make the salad, discard the tough stems from the arugula and mâche and put the leaves in a large salad bowl. Add the onion.

2. In a small baking dish, warm the goat cheese in the oven for 5 to 6 minutes.

3. Whisk together the vinaigrette ingredients in a measuring cup or small bowl until thickened. Pour over the salad and toss well to coat. Divide the salad among 4 salad plates. Crumble warm goat cheese atop each portion and serve immediately.

*Tolerance is the posture and cordial effort to understand another's beliefs, practices, and habits without necessarily sharing or accepting them.*

Joshua Liebman

# St. Joaquim Salad

*St. Joaquim was known to be the father of the Virgin Mary. His feast is kept on July 26, as is the feast of the Virgin Mary's mother, St. Anne.*

MAKES 6 SERVINGS

1 head cauliflower

6 large beets, trimmed

$1/2$ pound very thin string beans *(haricots verts)*, ends trimmed off

30 cherry tomatoes

$1^1/2$ cup Aioli Mayonnaise (page 239), prepared ahead and refrigerated until serving time

2 shallots, finely chopped

Leaves from 1 bunch fresh Italian parsley, finely chopped

1. Trim the cauliflower and separate the florets. Cook them in boiling salted water for 4 to 5 minutes maximum, until crisp-tender. Drain, then rinse under cold running water. Drain them again, shaking the colander or strainer. Set aside.

2. Cook the beets whole in boiling water for about 10 minutes, until crisp-tender. Drain and, when cool enough to handle, peel, then cut into cubes. Set aside separately from the cauliflower.

3. Cook the string beans in boiling salted water for 4 to 5 minutes until tender. Drain, then rinse under cold running water. Drain again, shaking the colander or strainer well. Set aside separately from the other vegetables.

4. On each of 6 salad plates, place a small amount of cauliflower near an edge. Next to it place an equal amount of beets. Next to those, set down a small pile of beans and then at least 5 cherry tomatoes. Place about $1/4$ cup of the mayonnaise in the center of the vegetables. Sprinkle the shallots on top of the beets and beans. Sprinkle the parsley on top of the cauliflower and tomatoes. Serve immediately as an appetizer.

# St. Anne Salad

*St. Anne is the mother of the Virgin Mary and grandmother of Christ. Her feast is kept on July 26.*

MAKES 6 TO 8 SERVINGS

*Salad*

½ pound sprouted wheat berries (available in health food stores and large supermarkets, in the Asian section)

2 cups water

Pinch of salt

½ pound dried black lentils (French, if possible), picked over and rinsed

1 medium-size Vidalia or another sweet onion, finely chopped

1 small bunch radishes, trimmed and thinly sliced

*Dressing*

½ cup plus 2 tablespoons hazelnut oil

5 teaspoons fresh lime juice

1 tablespoon prepared chili sauce

2 teaspoons caraway seeds

1 teaspoon paprika

Salt and freshly ground black pepper to taste

8 fresh spearmint leaves, finely chopped, for garnish

1. To make the salad, combine the wheat berries and water in a large saucepan. Add the salt and bring to a gentle boil over medium-low heat; let it continue to bubble for about 15 minutes. Drain, then rinse the wheat berries under cold running water and drain again, shaking the colander well. Set aside.

2. While the wheat berries are cooking, cook the lentils in boiling salted water until tender, 15 to 20 minutes. Drain, then rinse under cold running water and drain again, shaking the colander well.

3. In a large salad bowl, combine the wheat berries, lentils, onion, and radishes, mix gently, and refrigerate for at least 2 hours.

4. When ready to serve, whisk the dressing ingredients together in a measuring cup or small bowl until well blended. Pour over the salad and toss gently to coat well. Add the spearmint, mix well again, and serve immediately.

*Twelve Months of Monastery Salads*

# STUFFED MELON SALAD

*This dish makes an excellent and a complete lunch.*

*Salad*

2 small ripe melons of your choice

1½ cups cottage cheese

½ cup chopped walnuts

½ cup seedless raisins

¼ teaspoon ground nutmeg

A few fresh mint leaves, finely chopped

*Dressing*

½ cup half-and-half

½ teaspoon ground nutmeg

1 teaspoon paprika

1 teaspoon fresh lemon juice

1 tablespoon plus 1 teaspoon honey

Pinch of white pepper

1. To make the salad, cut the melons in half lengthwise and scoop out the seeds. Keep refrigerated until ready to serve.
2. In a deep bowl, combine the cottage cheese, walnuts, raisins, nutmeg, and mint and mix well with a fork.
3. In a blender, whirl the dressing ingredients until smooth. Check and adjust the seasonings.
4. When ready to serve, take the melons out of refrigerator. Fill their cavities with the cottage cheese mixture. Pour the dressing evenly over the 4 portions and serve immediately.

*Stewardship is the acceptance from God of personal responsibility for all of life and life's affairs.*

Roswell C. Long

# SUMMER FRUIT PLATTER

*D*uring *the long summer days and warm evenings, nothing is more appetizing or refreshing than this wonderful combination of fresh fruits. It is a basic fruit salad, simple to prepare and very healthy. Use a melon baller to make the melon balls.*

MAKES 6 TO 8 SERVINGS

1 head lettuce of your choice

2 cups plain yogurt, and more if needed

2 cups seedless watermelon balls

2 cups seedless melon balls

4 oranges, peeled, with white pith removed, separated into segments, and cut in half

4 ripe peaches, peeled, pitted, and thickly sliced

2 cups fresh blueberries, picked over for stems

2 cups fresh raspberries

Fresh lemon juice, as needed

1. Arrange the lettuce leaves on a large serving platter. Spoon the yogurt into a bowl and place in the center. Around the bowl arrange the watermelon, melon, oranges, peaches, blueberries, and raspberries. Drizzle lemon juice over the melons, peaches, and blueberries.

2. Pass the platter around as a dessert and let each diner help himself or herself.

*I am bending my knee*
*In the eye of the Father who created me,*
*In the eye of the Son who purchased me,*
*In the eye of the Spirit who cleansed me,*
*In friendship and affection.*
*Through Thine own Anointed One, O God,*
*Bestow upon us fullness in our need.*

Celtic prayer

# AUGUST

Spicy Black Bean Salad, Mexican Style  134

Salade Niçoise  135

Spanish Salad (Ensalada Española)  136

Transfiguration Salad  137

Gazpacho Salad  138

Israeli Salad  139

Mixed Jicama Salad  140

Rotelle in Spicy Napoleon Sauce  141

Italian Tomato Salad (Insalata di Pomodoro)  142

Tomato, Onion, and Mozzarella Salad  143

Mixed Green Salad Provençal
(Salade Mixte à la Provençale)  144

Salade des Crudités  145

Assumpta Salad  146

Regina Salad  147

St. Fiacre Salad  148

Riviera Cantaloupe Salad  149

Peach and Chicory Salad  150

Kiwi and Peach Salad  151

Summertime Salad  152

# Spicy Black Bean Salad, Mexican Style

### Makes 6 servings

## Salad

One 15.5-ounce can black beans, drained, rinsed under cold running water, and thoroughly drained again

4 ears corn, husked, cooked in boiling water for 5 minutes, drained, and kernels cut off

2 celery stalks, thinly sliced

1 medium-size green bell pepper, seeded and coarsely chopped

1 small chile pepper (optional), seeded and coarsely chopped

1 medium-size red onion, finely chopped

1/3 cup finely chopped fresh cilantro

## Dressing

1/4 cup extra virgin olive oil

1/4 cup fresh lime juice

1 garlic clove, minced

Pinch of ground cumin

Salt and freshly ground black pepper to taste

1 head Boston lettuce, separated into leaves

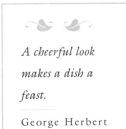

*A cheerful look makes a dish a feast.*

George Herbert

*Twelve Months of Monastery Salads*

1. In a large salad bowl, combine the salad ingredients and mix well. Cover and refrigerate for 2 hours.
2. One hour before serving, whisk the dressing ingredients together in a measuring cup or small bowl. Allow it to stand for at least 1 hour so the garlic flavor has time to develop.
3. When ready to serve, pour the dressing over the salad and toss to coat. Arrange 2 or 3 lettuce leaves on each salad plate. Spoon out the salad in equal portions on top of the lettuce and serve immediately.

# SALADE NIÇOISE

*Salad*

1 large head Boston lettuce, separated into leaves

6 ripe plum tomatoes, cut into wedges

1 large cucumber, peeled, seeded, and cubed

2 green bell peppers, seeded and cut into long, thin strips

1 large red onion, thinly sliced

One 6-ounce can tuna, drained and coarsely chopped

1/2 cup niçoise olives, drained and pitted

4 hard-boiled eggs, peeled and cut into wedges

1/4 cup packed fresh basil leaves, finely chopped

1/4 cup packed fresh Italian parsley leaves, finely chopped

*Vinaigrette*

1/2 cup plus 2 tablespoons extra virgin olive oil

2 tablespoons tarragon vinegar

Salt and freshly ground black pepper to taste

1. To assemble the salad, arrange the lettuce leaves in a circle on a large serving platter. Place the tomatoes, cucumber, peppers, and onion on top of the lettuce in that order, following the circular shape of the lettuce and leaving the center uncovered. Fill the center with the chunks of tuna, surrounded by the olives. Place the egg wedges all around the salad border. Sprinkle the herbs over the whole salad.

2. Just before serving, whisk the vinaigrette ingredients together in a measuring cup or small bowl until thickened and drizzle over the entire salad. Gently toss the tomato, cucumber, pepper, and onion without disturbing the rest. Serve immediately at room temperature.

*We seek God until God finds us.*

Madeleine L'Engle

# SPANISH SALAD

## (*Ensalada Española*)

### *Salad*

6 ripe tomatoes, cut into wedges

1 medium-size red bell pepper, seeded and cut into
long, thin strips

1 medium-size yellow bell pepper, seeded and cut
into long, thin strips

2 medium-size green bell peppers, seeded and cut
into long, thin strips

1 medium-size red onion, thinly sliced

2 small cucumbers, peeled and cut into thin rounds

1/2 cup pitted green olives, drained

### *Vinaigrette*

1/2 cup extra virgin olive oil (preferably Spanish)

1/4 cup Spanish sherry vinegar (preferably Jerez)

Salt and freshly ground black pepper to taste

Pinch of paprika

1. To assemble the salad, put the tomatoes, bell peppers, onion, cucumbers, and olives in a large salad bowl. (If you wish, before adding the onion to the salad, put it in a bowl filled with hot water for about 3 minutes to take away the sting. Drain and add to the salad.)
2. Whisk the vinaigrette ingredients together in a measuring cup or small bowl until thickened.
3. Just before serving, pour the vinaigrette over the salad, toss lightly to coat evenly, and serve at room temperature.

*My salad days,*
*When I was green in judgment, cold in blood,*
*To say as I said then!*

Shakespeare

# TRANSFIGURATION SALAD

*This salad should always be served cold. It is excellent for a picnic or a meal outdoors. We prepare this salad here at the monastery on special festive days, such as the Feast of the Transfiguration of the Lord on August 6, hence its name.*

MAKES 6 TO 8 SERVINGS

*Salad*

4 cups water

1 cup wild rice

One 15.5-ounce can chickpeas, drained and rinsed

1 small red onion, finely chopped

2 celery stalks, thinly sliced

1 cup cherry tomatoes

*Dressing*

¼ cup olive oil

¼ cup hazelnut oil

¼ cup cider vinegar or white wine vinegar

5 tablespoons low-fat sour cream

3 tablespoons sweet pickle relish

1 teaspoon sugar

Salt and freshly ground black pepper to taste


Finely chopped fresh Italian parsley for garnish

1. To make the salad, bring the water to a boil in a medium-size saucepan. Rinse the wild rice under cold running water, then add it to the boiling water. Cover and simmer over medium-low heat until the water is absorbed and the rice is tender, 30 to 40 minutes. Allow it to cool.

2. Put the rice in a deep salad bowl. Add the chickpeas, onion, celery, and cherry tomatoes and toss to combine.

3. Combine the dressing ingredients in a blender and whirl to a smooth and uniform consistency. Pour the dressing over the salad and toss to coat everything evenly.

4. Refrigerate for at least 2 hours before serving. Just before serving, sprinkle the parsley on top.

# GAZPACHO SALAD

This salad makes an excellent appetizer on a hot summer day. It can also be served alongside meat dishes.

MAKES 6 SERVINGS

## Salad

6 plum tomatoes, quartered

3 medium-size green bell peppers, seeded and cut into long, thin strips

1 medium-size red onion, thinly sliced

2 medium-size cucumbers, peeled (if not fresh from the garden) and cut into thin rounds

18 pitted green olives, coarsely chopped

1 garlic clove, minced

2 small ripe but firm avocados

Leaves from 1 small bunch fresh cilantro or Italian parsley, finely chopped

## Vinaigrette

⅓ cup extra virgin Spanish or another olive oil

¼ cup Spanish sherry vinegar (preferably Jerez) or red wine vinegar

Salt and freshly ground black pepper to taste

1. To assemble the salad, put the tomatoes, bell peppers, onion, cucumbers, olives, and garlic in a good-size salad bowl. Refrigerate for at least 2 hours.
2. Just before serving, peel and pit the avocados, slice, and add to the salad, along with half of the cilantro. Toss gently.
3. Whisk the vinaigrette ingredients together in a measuring cup or small bowl until thickened, pour over the salad, and toss again until everything is well coated. Divide the salad equally among 6 bowls. Garnish with the remaining cilantro and serve immediately.

# ISRAELI SALAD

*hough I recommend serving this cold, it is also nice served at room temperature, especially during the cold weather months. A friend who lives in Israel shared this recipe with me, and I have adapted it a bit for ingredients more commonly found here.*

MAKES 6 SERVINGS

## *Salad*

6 red radishes, trimmed and thinly sliced

4 pickling cucumbers (like Kirby), diced

2 medium-size cucumbers, peeled, seeded, and diced

6 ripe plum tomatoes, quartered

3 scallions (white and light green parts), chopped

12 pitted green olives, coarsely chopped

4 teaspoons capers, drained

## *Dressing*

7 tablespoons extra virgin olive oil

2 tablespoons fresh lemon juice

Salt and freshly ground black pepper to taste

Dash of cayenne pepper

Leaves from 1 small bunch fresh Italian parsley or chervil, finely chopped, for garnish

1. To assemble the salad, put the radishes, cucumbers, tomatoes, scallions, olives, and capers in a good-size salad bowl. Genty mix together and refrigerate for 1 to 2 hours maximum.

2. Just before serving, whisk the dressing ingredients together in a measuring cup or small bowl until thickened and pour over the salad. Toss gently to coat everything evenly, and divide the salad among 6 salad plates. Sprinkle with the chopped parsley and serve immediately.

*God respects me when I work, but he loves me when I sing.*

Rabindranath Tagore

# Mixed Jicama Salad

*his salad may be served as an appetizer or after the main course.*

## Salad

1 jicama (about 1 pound), peeled and shredded

4 small pickling cucumbers (like Kirby), cut into matchsticks

2 medium-size green bell peppers, seeded and cut into long, thin strips

2 medium-size apples, peeled, cored, and cut into matchsticks

1 tablespoon fresh lemon juice

6 fresh mint leaves, cut into thin strips

## Dressing

¼ cup extra virgin olive oil

2 teaspoons fresh lemon juice

2 teaspoons cider vinegar

Salt and freshly ground black pepper to taste

1. To assemble the salad, in a large salad bowl, combine the jicama, cucumbers, peppers, apples, and lemon juice. Toss gently to combine, cover, and refrigerate for 1 to 2 hours, until ready to serve. Just before serving, add the mint.

2. Whisk the dressing ingredients together in a measuring cup or small bowl until thickened, and pour over the salad. Toss lightly, making sure everything is evenly coated. Serve immediately.

# ROTELLE IN SPICY NAPOLEON SAUCE

1 pound rotelle pasta

One 1-pound package frozen peas

1 small Vidalia or another sweet onion, finely
  chopped

2/3 cup Spicy Napoleon Sauce (page 244)

1. Cook the rotelle in boiling salted water until *al dente*. Do not overcook. Drain, then rinse under cold running water until cool. Shake well in the colander and put in a deep salad bowl.

2. Cook the peas in boiling salted water following the instructions on the package. Do not overcook. Drain, then rinse under cold running water. Add the drained peas to the salad bowl. Add the onion. Pour the sauce over the salad and toss gently until everything is evenly coated.

3. Chill the salad in the refrigerator for at least 3 hours. Serve cold.

> *Time is a three-fold present: the present as we experience it, the past as a present memory, and the future as a present expectation.*
>
> St. Augustine of Hippo

# ITALIAN TOMATO SALAD

*(Insalata di Pomodoro)*

MAKES 6 SERVINGS

*Salad*

**3 large ripe red tomatoes, thickly sliced**

**3 large ripe yellow tomatoes, thickly sliced**

**1 medium-size red onion, thinly sliced**

**Handful of chopped fresh basil**

*Dressing*

**⅓ cup extra virgin olive oil, or more to taste**

**2 tablespoons fresh lemon juice**

**Salt and freshly ground black pepper to taste**

1. To make the salad, arrange the tomato slices on 6 salad plates in a decorative fashion, combining the red and yellow tomatoes. Distribute some of the onion slices on top of each serving. Do the same with the basil.

2. Whisk together the dressing ingredients in a measuring cup or small bowl until thickened, then drizzle over each serving. Serve immediately at room temperature.

*God far exceeds all words that we can here express,*
*In silence He is heard, in silence worshiped best.*

Angelus Silesius

# TOMATO, ONION, AND MOZZARELLA SALAD

*This dish is an excellent appetizer for lunch or supper.*

MAKES 6 TO 8 SERVINGS

6 large ripe red tomatoes, sliced

3 large ripe yellow tomatoes, sliced

1 medium-size red onion, thinly sliced

16 leaves fresh basil, or more to taste

1/2 pound fresh mozzarella cheese, sliced

Extra virgin olive oil to taste

Balsamic vinegar to taste

Sea salt and freshly ground black pepper to taste

Black olives, 4 per plate (optional), for garnish

1. Arrange the tomato slices on 6 or 8 salad plates, placing some red and some yellow on each plate. Over the tomatoes layer the onion slices, basil leaves, and mozzarella.

2. Just before serving, lightly sprinkle each serving with some olive oil and balsamic vinegar to taste. Sprinkle with a bit of sea salt and black pepper according to taste. Add 4 olives to each plate, if desired.

*August*

# MIXED GREEN SALAD PROVENÇAL

## (Salade Mixte à la Provençale)

*This salad is best served after the main course, as a transition to the dessert. In France it is often accompanied by an assortment of local cheeses.*

**MAKES 6 SERVINGS**

### Salad

1 head baby chicory (frisée), torn into bite-size pieces

1 bunch arugula, stems trimmed off

1 small bunch watercress, stems trimmed off, and cut into bite-size pieces

1 Belgian endive, leaves separated and torn into bite-size pieces

### Vinaigrette

1/4 cup extra virgin olive oil

3 tablespoons Raspberry-Scented Vinegar (page 236)

1 tablespoon Dijon, Meaux, or another French mustard

Salt and freshly ground black pepper to taste

1/4 cup minced fresh chervil for garnish

1. Combine the salad greens in a good-size salad bowl. Toss until well mixed.
2. Just before serving, whisk together the vinaigrette ingredients in a measuring cup or small bowl until thickened. Pour over the salad and toss lightly until the greens are evenly coated. Sprinkle with the chervil and serve immediately.

*To invite people to dine with us is to make ourselves responsible for their well-being for as long as they are under our roof.*

Anthelme Brillat-Savarin

# SALADE DES CRUDITÉS

*his sort of salad is usually served in France at the beginning of the meal, as a first course, especially during the summer months. It takes the place of the soup. Served informally from a platter that is passed around, it enhances the conviviality of the group gathered at the table.*

MAKES 6 TO 8 SERVINGS

## Salad

4 medium-size ripe tomatoes, sliced

1 good-size cucumber, peeled, seeded, and cut into small dice

1 red bell pepper, seeded and cut into small dice

1 green bell pepper, seeded and cut into small dice

1 medium-size onion, finely chopped

1 small head white or red cabbage, cored and cut into thin ribbons

4 medium-size carrots, peeled and cut into matchsticks

## Dressing

1 to 1¼ cups low-fat plain yogurt, to your taste

6 tablespoons mayonnaise (store-bought is fine, low-fat if you prefer)

¼ cup extra virgin olive oil

2 tablespoons fresh lemon juice

2 tablespoons cider vinegar

1 teaspoon paprika

1 tablespoon Dijon, Meaux, or another French mustard

Salt and white pepper to taste

Leaves from 1 small bunch fresh chervil or Italian parsley, finely chopped, for garnish

1. Choose a large platter to present this dish. To assemble, on one "corner" carefully arrange the tomatoes. Place the cucumber, peppers, and onion in a medium-size bowl. Mix well, then place on another corner of the platter, in the bowl. Place the cabbage on a third corner and the carrots on a fourth. This should be done in a decorative fashion according to the colors of the vegetables, so it entices the eyes. Leave a place in the center for the dressing. Just before serving, sprinkle the chervil on top of the vegetables.

2. Whirl the dressing ingredients in a blender for a few seconds until smooth. Pour into a small bowl and place in the center of the platter with a small serving spoon in it. Add a large serving spoon and fork to the platter and carry it to the table.

# ASSUMPTA SALAD

*his enticing salad is always served as an appetizer. It is one of our favorites for the feasts of Our Lady, and we especially like it on the Feast of the Assumption on August 15, when garden tomatoes are at their best.*

## Vinaigrette

½ cup plus 2 tablespoons extra virgin olive oil

5 tablespoons red wine vinegar

1 garlic clove, minced

Salt and freshly ground black pepper to taste

## Salad

8 medium-size ripe tomatoes, sliced

1 red onion, finely chopped

1 cup pitted black olives, drained

⅓ cup chopped fresh basil

¼ cup chopped fresh oregano

¼ cup chopped fresh Italian parsley

1 cup cubed feta cheese

1. Whisk the vinaigrette ingredients together in a measuring cup or small bowl until thickened. Let stand for 1 hour before using.
2. To assemble the salad, arrange the tomato slices on 6 to 8 salad plates. Sprinkle the chopped onion over the tomatoes and distribute the olives among them. Sprinkle the herbs evenly over the tomatoes. Place a few feta cheese cubes in the center of each dish.
3. Just before serving, whisk the vinaigrette again, then drizzle evenly over each serving and serve immediately.

*To sleep easy all*
*night,*
*let your supper be*
*light.*
*Or else you'll*
*complain*
*Of a stomach in*
*pain.*

Mother Goose

# REGINA SALAD

On August 22, we celebrate the feast of Maria Regina, Mary, the Queen of Heaven and Earth. This is a quick and easy salad to prepare. It can accompany the main course or be served afterward. It is also perfect for a simple picnic; carry the vinaigrette separately and add it to the salad just before serving.

MAKES 6 SERVINGS

### Salad

1 heart of romaine lettuce, torn into bite-size pieces

6 plum tomatoes, quartered

1 medium-size red onion, finely chopped

1 cup green grapes (seedless are best)

### Vinaigrette

⅓ cup extra virgin olive oil

4 teaspoons red wine vinegar

Salt and freshly ground black pepper to taste

6 tablespoons freshly grated Parmesan cheese for garnish

1. To assemble the salad, put the lettuce, tomatoes, onion, and grapes in a large salad bowl and chill for 1 hour.
2. Just before serving, remove the bowl from the refrigerator. Quickly whisk the vinaigrette ingredients together in a measuring cup or small bowl until thickened. Pour atop the salad and toss gently to coat everything. Sprinkle the top of the salad with the Parmesan and serve immediately.

# St. Fiacre Salad

*St. Fiacre is the patron saint of gardeners. He was an Irish monk who emigrated to France, where he became famous for his gardens. His feast day is kept on August 30.*

## Salad

1½ cups string beans, ends trimmed off, cooked in boiling water until crisp-tender, and drained

2 fennel bulbs, stalks discarded and bulbs thinly sliced lengthwise

4 medium-size ripe tomatoes, sliced

2 ripe but firm avocados, peeled, pitted, and cubed

1 medium-size red onion, thinly sliced

2 green bell peppers, seeded and sliced into long, thin strips

2 tablespoons fresh lemon juice

## Vinaigrette

⅓ cup extra virgin olive oil

¼ cup red wine vinegar

Salt and freshly ground black pepper to taste

Leaves from 1 bunch fresh cilantro, finely chopped, for garnish

1. To assemble the salad, combine the string beans, fennel, tomatoes, avocados, onion, and peppers in a large salad bowl. Sprinkle with the lemon juice and toss lightly.

2. Whisk the vinaigrette ingredients together in a measuring cup or small bowl until thickened. Add more oil or vinegar if needed. Pour over the salad and toss to coat evenly. Sprinkle with the cilantro and serve immediately.

# RIVIERA CANTALOUPE SALAD

*S*erve this appetizing salad before the main course or as a dessert.

MAKES 6 TO 8 SERVINGS

2 small to medium-size ripe cantaloupes, seeded, and flesh cut from the rind and into bite-size chunks

1½ cups ripe but firm blueberries, picked over for stems, or seedless purple grapes

2 tablespoons fresh lemon juice

⅓ cup sweet or dry sherry

3 tablespoons sugar

8 fresh mint leaves, finely shredded

One 8-ounce container (1 cup) plain or vanilla low-fat yogurt for garnish

1. Put the cantaloupe chunks in a large glass salad bowl. Add the blueberries and lemon juice and toss lightly. Refrigerate for 1 hour.

2. One hour, more or less, prior to serving, pour the sherry into the salad bowl. Add the sugar and half of the mint leaves, toss to coat everything well, and refrigerate.

3. Just before serving, divide the fruit salad among 6 to 8 small bowls (preferably glass). Spoon about 2 tablespoons of yogurt in the center of each. Sprinkle the remaining mint on top and serve immediately.

---

*It requires grace to turn a person into a saint, and anyone who doubts it does not know what a saint or what a person is.*

Pascal

# PEACH AND CHICORY SALAD

*Serve this salad any time and on any occasion, particularly when peaches are in season. It is always delicious!*

MAKES 6 SERVINGS

### Salad

1 small head baby chicory (frisée), torn into
   bite-size pieces

6 ripe peaches, peeled, pitted, and sliced lengthwise

One 1.5-ounce box golden raisins

$\frac{1}{2}$ cup chopped walnuts

### Dressing

$\frac{1}{3}$ cup hazelnut oil

$\frac{1}{4}$ cup white wine vinegar

Salt and freshly ground black pepper to taste

$\frac{1}{4}$ pound goat cheese, crumbled, for garnish

1. In a large salad bowl, combine the chicory, peaches, raisins, and walnuts. Mix well.
2. Just before serving, whisk the dressing ingredients together in a measuring cup or small bowl and pour over the salad. Toss to coat everything evenly. Distribute the salad equally among 6 salad plates. Garnish with the crumbled goat cheese and serve immediately.

# KIWI AND PEACH SALAD

### Salad

4 kiwis, peeled and cut into equal rounds

4 ripe peaches, peeled, pitted, and cut into equal slices

1 cup fresh blueberries, picked over for stems

2 tablespoons fresh lemon juice

### Dressing

1 cup low-fat sour cream or, even better, crème fraîche

¼ cup honey

¼ cup port wine

1 tablespoon sugar

1. To assemble the salad, arrange the sliced kiwis in a circle around the outer edge of each of 4 salad plates. In a deep bowl, mix together the peaches, blueberries, and lemon juice. Toss gently. Place some of this mixture in the center of each plate.

2. Whisk the dressing ingredients together in a measuring cup or medium-size bowl until smooth. Just before serving, pour some of the dressing evenly over the peach mixture on each plate and serve immediately.

*Therefore I say that we must learn to look through every gift and every event to God and never be content with the thing itself.*

Meister Eckehart

# SUMMERTIME SALAD

*W*e prepare this appetizing summer salad when melons and blueberries are in season. It is best served as a dessert.

### Salad

1 ripe cantaloupe, seeded and flesh cut from the rind and into bite-size chunks

1 medium-size ripe watermelon, seeded and flesh cut from the rind and into bite-size chunks

1 cup fresh blueberries, picked over for stems

### Dressing

5 tablespoons orange juice

3 tablespoons fresh lemon juice

$\frac{1}{4}$ cup honey

$\frac{1}{4}$ cup dry white wine

8 fresh mint leaves, finely chopped, for garnish

1. To assemble the salad, put the cantaloupe and watermelon chunks in a large glass bowl. Add the blueberries and mix well. Refrigerate until ready to serve.

2. Whirl the dressing ingredients in a blender until smooth. Add more of each ingredient to taste, if needed. Pour the dressing over the salad and toss to coat everything evenly. Refrigerate for another half hour before serving chilled, garnished with the mint.

*Make your work of love a beautiful thing: want nothing else, fear nothing else, and let love be free to become what love truly is.*

Hadewijch of Antwerp

# SEPTEMBER

MADRID MIXED SALAD (*ENSALADA MIXTA DE MADRID*)    154

HORIATIKI GREEK SALAD    155

*SALADE COMPOSÉE*    156

POTATO SALAD MONT-BLANC    157

BLACK-EYED PEA SALAD, PORTUGUESE STYLE    158

TUSCAN STUFFED TOMATO SALAD    159

BROCCOLI, CAULIFLOWER, AND JICAMA IN YOGURT DRESSING    160

CABBAGE, APPLE, AND PINEAPPLE SLAW    161

BABY BEET, POTATO, AND ONION SALAD    162

GUACAMOLE SALAD    163

CHICKPEA SALAD    164

LATE-SUMMER TOMATO AND PARSLEY SALAD    165

POLE BEAN SALAD    166

*SALADE SAVOYARDE*    167

ST. BASIL MACARONI SALAD    168

ST. HILDEGARDE'S SALAD    169

ST. MICHAEL'S SALAD    170

BERRIED SMOKED SALMON SALAD    171

TANGY FRUIT SALAD    172

FRUIT RELISH SALAD    173

HEAVENLY FRUIT SALAD WITH CAMEMBERT    174

# MADRID MIXED SALAD

## (Ensalada Mixta de Madrid)

MAKES 6 SERVINGS

### Vinaigrette

½ cup extra virgin olive oil (preferably Spanish)

¼ cup Spanish sherry vinegar (preferably Jerez)

1 garlic clove, finely minced

Salt and freshly ground black pepper to taste

### Salad

1 head Boston or other butterhead lettuce

One 6-ounce can tuna, drained and coarsely chopped

1 medium-size Spanish onion, cut in half and sliced into half-moons

3 medium-size ripe tomatoes, cut into wedges

½ cup pitted green olives, drained

6 green or white asparagus (optional), bottoms trimmed off, steamed until crisp-tender, and cut into 2-inch lengths

3 hard-boiled eggs, peeled and sliced

*Loving-kindness is the better part of goodness.*

W. Somerset Maugham

1. Whisk the vinaigrette ingredients together in a measuring cup or small bowl until thickened, and let stand for at least 20 minutes so the garlic flavor can develop.

2. To make the salad, wash and thoroughly drain the lettuce leaves. Cut them in half and put them in a large salad bowl. Add the remaining ingredients, except the eggs.

3. Just before serving, pour the vinaigrette over the salad and toss lightly to coat everything. Arrange the egg slices over the top and serve immediately.

# HORIATIKI GREEK SALAD

*Salad*

1 head tender escarole

8 plum tomatoes, cut lengthwise into thin wedges

1 red onion, thinly sliced

$1/2$ pound feta cheese, cubed

16 black olives (preferably Kalamata), pitted

A few sprigs fresh Italian parsley, finely chopped

*Dressing*

$1/3$ cup extra virgin olive oil

$1/4$ cup fresh lemon juice

Salt and freshly ground black pepper to taste

1. To assemble the salad, tear the escarole into bite-size pieces and put in a large salad bowl. Add the tomatoes, onion, feta, olives, and parsley and toss the salad lightly.
2. Just before serving, whisk the dressing ingredients together in a measuring cup or small bowl until thickened, and pour it over the salad. Toss the salad until coated and serve immediately.

# SALADE COMPOSÉE

his French salad is generally served as an appetizer.

MAKES 6 SERVINGS

½ pound very thin string beans *(haricots verts)*, ends trimmed off

12 radishes, trimmed and cut into roses

3 carrots, peeled and thinly shredded

1 small head baby chicory (frisée), separated into leaves and cut in half

4 medium-size ripe tomatoes, sliced

18 pitted green or black olives

1 cup Aioli Mayonnaise (page 239), prepared ahead of time and refrigerated until ready to use

1. Bring a medium-size saucepan of salted water to a boil, add the string beans, and cook, uncovered, for 4 to 5 minutes maximum. Drain, cool under cold running water, and drain again.

2. Just prior to serving, assemble the salad: On each of 6 individual salad plates, arrange the vegetables in a decorative fashion, leaving room in the center for a generous dollop of aioli. I suggest this order for the vegetables: string beans, radishes, carrots, chicory, tomatoes, olives.

3. Place an equal amount of aioli in the center of each plate and serve immediately.

*Lettuce is the jewel of the salad garden because it is the very heart of the salad bowl itself.*

Sam Bittman

# POTATO SALAD MONT-BLANC

## *Salad*

8 medium-size potatoes, peeled and cubed

4 hard-boiled eggs, peeled and coarsely chopped

## *Dressing*

One 8-ounce container (1 cup) low-fat sour cream

2 scallions, finely chopped

3 tablespoons finely chopped fresh Italian parsley

3 tablespoons finely chopped fresh tarragon

3 tablespoons finely chopped fresh mint

$1/4$ cup extra virgin olive oil

1 teaspoon fresh lemon juice

Salt and freshly ground black pepper to taste

1. To make the salad, cook the potatoes in a large saucepan of boiling salted water until tender. Do not overcook them; the potato cubes must remain firm. Drain, then rinse under cold running water and shake the colander well to remove as much water as possible. Put the potatoes in a good-size salad bowl. Add the chopped eggs and toss together a bit.

2. To make the dressing, put the sour cream in a deep bowl and add the remaining dressing ingredients. Blend well with a whisk or electric mixer. Taste and adjust the seasonings. Add to the potato-egg mixture and mix together to coat well. Cover and refrigerate for at least 2 hours before serving. Serve cold.

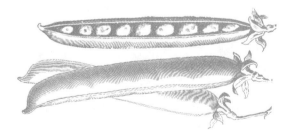

# BLACK-EYED PEA SALAD,
# PORTUGUESE STYLE

*I first tasted this delicious salad in the town of Funchal, on the Portuguese island of Madeira. This recipe is a re-creation from memory.*

MAKES 6 TO 8 SERVINGS

## Salad

1 pound dried black-eyed peas, picked over, or two 15-ounce cans black-eyed peas, drained and rinsed

6 medium-size potatoes, peeled and cubed

1 medium-size Vidalia onion, chopped

3 garlic cloves, minced

1/2 cup chopped fresh Italian parsley

## Dressing

1/2 cup extra virgin olive oil

1/4 cup white wine vinegar

1 teaspoon crumbled dried thyme or oregano

Sea salt and freshly ground black pepper to taste

2 hard-boiled eggs, peeled and finely chopped, for garnish

1. If using canned beans, skip this step. Soak the dried beans in water to cover (generously) for at least 3 to 4 hours. Drain, then put the beans in a large saucepan, add the water, and bring to a boil. Reduce the heat to medium and continue to cook until tender but not mushy, about 1 hour. Drain, then rinse under cold running water. Drain again thoroughly.

2. Meanwhile, cook the cubed potatoes in a large saucepan of boiling salted water for 5 to 6 minutes. They must remain firm and *al dente*. Drain and rinse under cold running water. Drain once more and put in a good-size ceramic bowl. Add the cooked peas, onion, and garlic and mix gently. Cover and refrigerate for a few hours. Just before serving, add the parsley and mix again.

3. Whisk together the dressing ingredients in a measuring cup or small bowl until thickened. Taste and adjust the seasonings. Pour over the salad and toss to coat. Sprinkle the eggs over the salad and serve immediately.

# TUSCAN STUFFED TOMATO SALAD

*his salad can be served as a delightful appetizer or after the main course. It is particularly suitable when tomatoes and fresh herbs are in season.*

MAKES 6 SERVINGS

12 medium-size ripe tomatoes

One 8-ounce container (1 cup) plain yogurt

¼ cup mayonnaise (store-bought is fine)

1 small cucumber, peeled, seeded, and finely chopped

1 teaspoon fresh lemon juice

1 small white or red onion or 2 shallots, finely chopped

1 tablespoon finely chopped fresh parsley

1 tablespoon finely chopped fresh chives

1 tablespoon finely chopped fresh dill

Freshly ground black pepper to taste

1 head Boston lettuce, separated into leaves

Extra virgin olive oil, as needed

1. Cut off the tomato tops with a small sharp knife. With a small spoon, gently scoop out the insides of each tomato without puncturing the skins. Lay the shells upside down to drain them thoroughly, about 10 minutes. Discard the insides or save to use in a sauce.

2. In a large bowl, mix together the yogurt and mayonnaise. Add the cucumber, lemon juice, onion, parsley, chives, and dill; season with pepper and blend together well. Carefully fill the tomato shells with the yogurt-vegetable mixture.

3. Place 2 or 3 lettuce leaves on each salad plate. Drizzle a few drops of olive oil on top of them. Place 2 stuffed tomatoes atop the lettuce on each plate and serve.

*Adopt the pace of nature, her secret is patience.*

Ralph Waldo Emerson

# BROCCOLI, CAULIFLOWER, AND JICAMA IN YOGURT DRESSING

*This salad is very nutritious and makes a pleasant warm weather appetizer.*

MAKES 6 TO 8 SERVINGS

### Salad

1 medium-size head broccoli, cut into bite-size florets

1 medium-size head cauliflower, cut into bite-size florets

1/2 jicama, peeled and coarsely shredded

1 medium-size cucumber, peeled, seeded, and cubed

2 tablespoons fresh lemon juice

### Dressing

One 8-ounce container (1 cup) plain yogurt

1 shallot, coarsely chopped

2 teaspoons finely chopped fresh dill

3 tablespoons finely chopped fresh Italian parsley

1/4 cup shelled natural pistachios, toasted in a dry skillet over medium heat until lightly browned and fragrant, then coarsely chopped

Salt and freshly ground black pepper to taste

1. To make the salad, cook the broccoli and cauliflower florets together in a large saucepan of boiling salted water for about 2 minutes. They must not overcook and should remain crisp-tender. Drain, then rinse under cold running water and drain again. Put the broccoli and cauliflower in a large salad bowl. Add the jicama, cucumber, and lemon juice and toss lightly. Cover and refrigerate while preparing the dressing.

2. To make the dressing, put the yogurt in a measuring cup or small bowl. Add the remaining dressing ingredients and whisk thoroughly. Taste and adjust the seasonings. Pour the dressing over the salad and mix gently to coat everything. Cover and refrigerate for 2 hours before serving.

# Cabbage, Apple, and Pineapple Slaw

*This is an excellent coleslaw for a summer picnic.*

MAKES 6 TO 8 SERVINGS

## Salad

1 small head green or red cabbage, cored and finely chopped

2 green apples, peeled, cored, quartered, and thinly sliced

One 8-ounce can juicy pineapple chunks, drained, reserving 2 tablespoons of the juice for the dressing, and coarsely chopped

1 small red onion, cut in half and thinly sliced into half-moons

One 1.5-ounce box golden raisins

1 fennel bulb, stalks discarded and bulb finely shredded

3 tablespoons fresh lemon juice

## Dressing

¼ cup mayonnaise (store-bought is fine)

¼ cup plain yogurt or mayonnaise

2 tablespoons reserved pineapple juice

1 teaspoon sugar

Dash of freshly ground black pepper to taste

1. Put the salad ingredients in a large salad bowl, setting aside the 2 tablespoons of pineapple juice, and mix gently. Cover and refrigerate while preparing the dressing.

2. Whisk together the dressing ingredients in a measuring cup or small bowl until smooth. Add to the salad and mix to coat well. Cover and refrigerate for several hours before serving.

*Economy is the art of making the most of life. The love of economy is the root of all virtue.*

George Bernard Shaw

# BABY BEET, POTATO, AND ONION SALAD

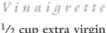 *his is an excellent appetizer any time of the year, but especially in the late days of summer, when baby beets and small potatoes are harvested from the garden.*

**MAKES 4 SERVINGS**

### Salad

12 very small beets

12 very small red potatoes, peeled

16 pearl onions, peeled

### Vinaigrette

1/2 cup extra virgin olive oil

3 tablespoons white wine or distilled vinegar

2 teaspoons Dijon, Meaux, or another French mustard

Salt and freshly ground black pepper to taste

6 tablespoons finely chopped fresh dill for garnish

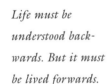

*Life must be understood backwards. But it must be lived forwards.*

Søren Kierkegaard

1. To make the salad, trim the beets at both ends. Cook them in a large saucepan of boiling salted water until tender, about 30 minutes. Drain and rinse under cold running water. Peel and set aside.

2. In two other saucepans of boiling water, cook the potatoes and onions separately for about 15 minutes. Do not overcook them; they should remain firm and whole. Drain and allow to cool.

3. When ready to serve, place the beets, potatoes, and onions in a deep salad bowl.

4. Whisk the vinaigrette ingredients together in a measuring cup or small bowl until thickened. Pour over the vegetables and toss gently to coat well. Garnish with the dill and serve immediately.

# Guacamole Salad

3 large ripe but firm avocados

1 large ripe tomato, peeled, seeded, and chopped

1 medium-size Vidalia onion, diced

1 small red bell pepper, seeded and diced

1 green bell pepper, seeded and diced

3 tablespoons finely chopped fresh cilantro

2 tablespoons sour cream or plain yogurt

2 tablespoons fresh lemon juice

Salt and freshly ground black pepper to taste

1. Remove the peels and pits of the avocados and mash them in a deep bowl. Add the tomato, onion, bell peppers, and cilantro and mix together well. Add the sour cream and lemon juice and season with salt and pepper. Mix together very well.

2. Cover, and place in the refrigerator until ready to serve, up to 3 hours.

# CHICKPEA SALAD

*This is a good salad to serve throughout the summer months.*

**MAKES 4 TO 6 SERVINGS**

*Salad*

2 cups freshly cooked chickpeas or two 15-ounce
    cans chickpeas, drained and rinsed

2 medium-size red bell peppers, seeded and diced

1 medium-size red onion, minced

2 celery stalks, thinly sliced

1 small cucumber, peeled, seeded, and cubed

*Dressing*

⅓ cup extra virgin olive oil

5 teaspoons fresh lemon juice

Salt and freshly ground black pepper to taste

Chopped fresh cilantro (optional) for garnish

1. To assemble the salad, put the chickpeas in a deep salad bowl. Add the remaining salad ingredients, mix well, cover, and place in the refrigerator for at least 2 hours.

2. Just before serving, whisk together the dressing ingredients in a measuring cup or small bowl until thickened. Pour over the salad, add the cilantro, if using, and toss gently to coat well. Serve immediately.

# LATE-SUMMER TOMATO AND PARSLEY SALAD

MAKES 6 SERVINGS

*Salad*

8 medium-size to large ripe tomatoes, cut into thin slices

1 small red onion, thinly sliced

Leaves from 1 bunch fresh Italian parsley

18 pitted green olives

*Vinaigrette*

6 tablespoons extra virgin olive oil

2 tablespoons balsamic vinegar

Salt and freshly ground black pepper to taste

2 hard-boiled eggs, peeled and chopped, for garnish

1. Put the tomatoes, onion, parsley, and olives in a good-size bowl.
2. Just before serving, whisk the vinaigrette ingredients together in a measuring cup or small bowl until thickened, pour over the salad, and gently toss until well coated. Divide the salad among 6 salad plates. Garnish the top of each serving with some of the chopped eggs and serve immediately.

*You give a little when you give of your possessions.*
*It is when you give of yourself that you truly give.*

Kahil Gibran

# POLE BEAN SALAD

*This is a terrific appetizer for lunch or brunch, especially during the summer and early fall months.*

MAKES 6 SERVINGS

### Salad

½ pound pole beans (such as Romano), ends
   trimmed off

6 medium-size ripe tomatoes, sliced

1 medium-size red onion, thinly sliced

### Vinaigrette

½ cup extra virgin olive oil

¼ cup red wine vinegar

Salt and freshly ground black pepper to taste

Chopped fresh basil for garnish

*Out of the kitchen
come the best tunes.*

Irish proverb

1. To make the salad, cook the beans in a large saucepan of salted water until crisp-tender, 4 to 5 minutes. Drain, rinse under cold running water, and drain again. Divide the beans among 6 salad plates, arranging them on one half of each dish. Place the tomato slices on the other half. Scatter the sliced onion over the tomatoes.

2. Just before serving, whisk the vinaigrette ingredients together in a measuring cup or small bowl until thickened, adding more oil and/or vinegar if necessary. Pour evenly over the salads. Sprinkle with basil and serve immediately.

# SALADE SAVOYARDE

*his excellent salad, which has its origins in the beautiful alpine area of Savoy in France, is a great choice for a picnic or outdoor party.*

MAKES 6 TO 8 SERVINGS

## *Salad*

1 small head cabbage, cored and very thinly sliced

4 medium-size carrots, peeled and cut into matchsticks

4 shallots, finely chopped

2 tart apples, peeled, cored, and cubed

¼ cup white wine vinegar or cider vinegar

2 teaspoons sugar

## *Dressing*

One 8-ounce container (1 cup) plain yogurt

⅓ cup low-fat mayonnaise

2 teaspoons chopped fresh chervil

Salt and freshly ground black pepper to taste

1. In a large salad bowl, combine the salad ingredients. Toss to mix well, cover the bowl with aluminum foil or a lid, and refrigerate for at least 3 hours.
2. Just before serving, whisk together the dressing ingredients in a measuring cup or small bowl until smooth and add it to the salad. Mix well until everything is evenly coated. Serve immediately or refrigerate until ready to serve, up to 4 hours.

*September*

# St. Basil Macaroni Salad

*S*t. Basil, who is called "the Great," was born in Asarea, in Asia Minor, to an old noble Christian family. Deeply moved by the example of the early Christian monks, he settled around Pontus, on the same peninsula, where he lived for a few years in the company of monks. To this day, his monastic rule continues to influence monks of the East and West. His feast day is celebrated on January 2.

MAKES 4 TO 6 SERVINGS

*Salad*

3/4 pound macaroni

One 10-ounce package frozen peas

1 medium-size to large yellow bell pepper

1 medium-size to large red bell pepper

1 medium-size to large red onion, chopped

2 gherkins or cornichons, thinly sliced

2 hard-boiled eggs, peeled and coarsely chopped

2 tablespoons capers, drained

*Dressing*

1/2 cup Aioli Mayonnaise (page 239)

1 tablespoon Dijon, Meaux, or another French mustard

1 tablespoon fresh lemon juice

Salt and freshly ground black pepper to taste

1. Preheat the oven to 400°F or preheat the broiler. Cook the macaroni in a large saucepan of boiling salted water until *al dente*; do not overcook. Drain, rinse under cold running water, and transfer to a deep salad bowl.

2. Cook the peas in a medium-size saucepan of boiling salted water until tender, about 3 minutes; do not overcook. Drain and add to the salad bowl.

3. Roast or broil the peppers, turning them a few times, until blackened all over. Put in a paper bag, close it, and let them cool in the bag for a few minutes. Remove from the bag carefully, peel their skins off, and wash under cold running water to remove any blackened bits. Pat dry with paper towels. Remove their stems, cut them in half, remove the seeds, slice into thin strips, and add to the salad bowl. Add the onion, eggs, and capers.

4. Combine the dressing ingredients. Whisk until well blended. Taste and adjust the seasonings, if necessary. Pour over the salad and stir until everything is evenly coated. Refrigerate for at least 3 hours before serving.

# ST. HILDEGARDE'S SALAD

*St. Hildegarde, remarkable for her visions as well as for her wisdom, was one of the most famous women of the Middle Ages. She wrote extensively about many subjects, from treatises on the Gospel to the natural sciences. She founded a monastery of Benedictine nuns on the shores of the Rhine River that exists to this day and has become famous for the quality of wine produced by the nuns there. St. Hildegarde's feast is on September 17.*

**MAKES 6 SERVINGS**

*Salad*

½ pound Belgian endives

½ pound Swiss cheese, cubed

⅓ cup chopped scallions

*Dressing*

⅓ cup mayonnaise, homemade (page 238) or
   store-bought

¼ cup heavy cream (optional)

1 teaspoon Dijon mustard

2 teaspoons fresh lemon juice

1 teaspoon dry white vermouth

1. To make the salad, separate the endives into leaves and cut into 1-inch-long pieces. Put in a salad bowl and add the cheese and scallions.

2. In a medium-size bowl, combine the dressing ingredients and, if you are using the cream, beat with an electric mixer until stiff peaks form. Pour over the salad, mix well to coat everything, and cover. Refrigerate for at least 1 hour before serving. Serve cold.

*Live within your harvest.*

Persian proverb

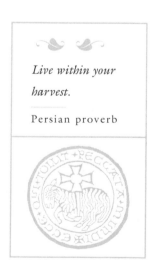

# ST. MICHAEL'S SALAD

*The feast of the three archangels—Michael, Raphael, and Gabriel—is celebrated on September 29. This salad is an excellent appetizer to serve with the late-harvest tomatoes of an Indian summer.*

MAKES 4 SERVINGS

4 large ripe but firm tomatoes

1 medium-size red onion, thinly sliced

Salt and freshly ground black pepper to taste

16 pitted green olives

4 slices mozzarella cheese, about $\frac{1}{4}$ inch thick

Handful of fresh basil leaves, coarsely chopped

Extra virgin olive oil to taste

Trim the ends of the tomatoes and cut into $\frac{1}{2}$-inch-thick slices. Arrange in circular patterns on 4 salad plates. Distribute the onions evenly over the tomatoes. Sprinkle salt and pepper over the tomatoes and onions. Place 4 olives on each plate. Place 1 mozzarella slice at the center. Sprinkle the basil evenly over each plate. Drizzle olive oil over the top and serve immediately.

*Our hearts are small, but prayer stretches them and makes them capable of containing God.*

St. John Vianney

# BERRIED SMOKED SALMON SALAD

*This light salad can be served as an appetizer or after the main course, as an interlude before dessert.*

MAKES 4 TO 6 SERVINGS

## Salad

1 medium-size head romaine lettuce, torn into
   bite-size pieces

8 ounces sliced smoked salmon, cut into 1/4-inch-
   wide strips

1 1/2 cups mixed fresh berries (such as blueberries,
   blackberries, and raspberries)

2 oranges, peeled, with white pith removed, cut
   crosswise into rounds, and quartered

3 scallions, thinly sliced

## Dressing

1/2 cup plus 2 tablespoons extra virgin olive oil

1/4 cup fresh lemon juice

1 tablespoon white wine vinegar

2 teaspoons honey mustard

Salt and freshly ground black pepper to taste

1. To assemble the salad, put the lettuce in a large salad bowl. Add the
   salmon, berries, oranges, and scallions and toss to mix well.

2. Whisk the dressing ingredients together in a measuring cup or small bowl
   until thickened. Pour the dressing over the salad and toss to coat everything evenly. Spoon the salad onto serving plates and serve immediately.

*September*

# TANGY FRUIT SALAD

*his interesting salad is particularly refreshing during the hot weather months, when it should be served very cold.*

**MAKES 6 SERVINGS**

### Salad

3 green apples, peeled, cored, and thinly sliced

3 tangerines, peeled, with white pith removed, and separated into segments

1 medium-size cucumber, peeled, seeded, and diced

¼ cup pecans, chopped

### Dressing

One 8-ounce container (1 cup) plain yogurt

2 tablespoons olive oil

2 teaspoons fresh lime juice

1 teaspoon paprika

1 teaspoon dry mustard

1 teaspoon sugar

Pinch of white pepper to taste

1 head Boston lettuce, separated into leaves

1. To assemble the salad, put the apples, tangerines, and cucumber in a large salad bowl. Add the pecans and toss. Refrigerate until ready to serve, at least 1 hour.
2. Combine the dressing ingredients in a blender and whirl until smooth. When ready to serve, pour over the salad and toss to coat. Line each of 6 salad plates with 2 or 3 lettuce leaves and put a portion of the salad on top.

*Whatsoever was the father of the disease, an ill diet was the mother.*

George Herbert

# FRUIT RELISH SALAD

*his salad is particularly appetizing in late summer, when fruits are at their peak. Serve it as a light dessert, following a good meal.*

**MAKES 6 TO 8 SERVINGS**

*Salad*

1 ripe melon, seeded and flesh cut away from the
   rind and into small cubes

4 ripe peaches, peeled, pitted, and coarsely chopped

1 cup fresh raspberries

1 cup seedless green grapes

1/2 cup sweetened or unsweetened shredded coconut

*Dressing*

1/2 cup fresh orange juice

3 tablespoons fresh lemon juice

1/4 cup honey

2 tablespoons peach or raspberry liqueur

2 tablespoons peach jam

1. To assemble the salad, in a large glass bowl, combine the fruit and coconut.
   Mix well and set aside.

2. Combine the dressing ingredients in a blender and whirl until smooth.
   Pour over the fruit salad and toss to coat evenly. Refrigerate for 2 to 3
   hours, and serve chilled.

*Good food should be grown on whole soil, be eaten whole, unprocessed,
and garden fresh.*

Helen and Scott Nearing

# HEAVENLY FRUIT SALAD WITH CAMEMBERT

*This salad is indeed heavenly and always served as a dessert. If you are unable to find Camembert, substitute Brie cheese.*

**MAKES 6 SERVINGS**

## Salad

12 fresh strawberries, hulled and cut in half

1½ cups fresh raspberries

1½ cups fresh blueberries, picked over for stems

4 medium-size pears, peeled, quartered, and cored

2 tablespoons fresh lemon juice

2 teaspoons sugar

## Dressing

½ cup dry white wine

3 tablespoons honey

2 tablespoons fresh lemon juice

2 tablespoons sugar (or more honey)

One 12-ounce wheel Camembert cheese, at room temperature, cut into 6 wedges

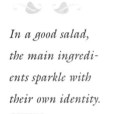

*In a good salad, the main ingredients sparkle with their own identity.*

Author unknown

1. To make the salad, combine all the fruit in a large glass bowl. Add the lemon juice and sugar, mix together gently to coat, cover, and refrigerate for 1 hour.
2. Combine the dressing ingredients in a blender and whirl until smooth. Pour over the salad and mix together gently until the salad is well coated. Cover and refrigerate for 1 more hour.
3. Just before serving, divide the salad equally among 6 salad plates. Place the fruit on one side of each plate and the Camembert on the other. Serve the salad chilled and the cheese at room temperature.

# OCTOBER

CHICKPEA SALAD, SPANISH STYLE  176

CRUNCHY COUSCOUS SALAD  177

DUTCHESS COUNTY CRISPY SALAD WITH BLUE CHEESE DRESSING  178

GREEN BEAN AND TOMATO SALAD  179

CHILLED AMBER SALAD  180

COOKED FENNEL SALAD  181

RED BEET SALAD WITH ROQUEFORT CHEESE  182

RUSSIAN FRUIT AND VEGETABLE SALAD  183

AVOCADO AND WATERCRESS SALAD  184

CHERRY TOMATOES AND BULGUR SALAD  185

PENNE SALAD  186

RIGATONI AND BROCCOLI SALAD  187

ORECCHIETTE, ARUGULA, AND RADICCHIO SALAD  188

*SALADE LANDAISE*  189

CARROT AND BLACK OLIVE SALAD
(*CAROTTES RAPÉES AUX OLIVES*)  190

POTATO SALAD HOLY ELDER SIMEON  191

ST. FRANCIS SALAD  192

RAINBOW SALAD  193

TUTTI-FRUTTI SALAD  194

PERSIMMON AND GREENS SALAD  195

# CHICKPEA SALAD, SPANISH STYLE

### MAKES 6 TO 8 SERVINGS

*Dressing*

¹/₃ cup extra virgin olive oil (preferably Spanish)

5 tablespoons fresh lemon juice

2 garlic cloves, minced

Salt and freshly ground black pepper to taste

*Salad*

2 cups dried chickpeas, rinsed, picked over, and if
time permits, soaked overnight in water to cover
generously, or 2 cups canned chickpeas

6 plum tomatoes, seeded and finely chopped

1 medium-size red onion, finely chopped

1 medium-size cucumber, peeled, seeded, and diced

12 pitted green or black olives, coarsely chopped

1 medium-size green bell pepper, seeded and diced

A few sprigs fresh Italian parsley, finely chopped,
for garnish

*God gives food to
every bird, but does
not throw it into
the nest.*

Montenegrin
proverb

1. Whisk together the dressing ingredients in a measuring cup or small bowl.
   Let it stand for at least 1 hour to let the garlic flavor develop.
2. If using dried chickpeas, cook them in boiling salted water until tender, 30
   to 40 minutes. Drain, then rinse under cold running water. Shake the
   colander or strainer well, then put them in a large salad bowl. (If you prefer
   canned chickpeas, drain and rinse them under cold running water to get rid
   of the tinny taste.)
3. Add the tomatoes, onion, cucumber, olives, and pepper and toss gently.
4. When ready to serve, pour the dressing over the salad and toss gently, making sure everything is evenly coated. Sprinkle with the chopped parsley and
   serve immediately.

# CRUNCHY COUSCOUS SALAD

*This is an excellent salad to serve at a party or large gathering of friends. It has the added advantage of keeping well, so that you can prepare it the day before or several hours ahead of time.*

MAKES 8 SERVINGS

*Salad*

2½ cups water

Pinch of salt

1 cup couscous

⅓ cup shelled fresh or frozen peas

⅓ cup chopped walnuts

⅓ cup chopped pecans

½ cup dark raisins

1 medium-size red onion, chopped

2 medium-size cucumbers, peeled, seeded, and
  cubed

A few fresh mint leaves, finely chopped

*Dressing*

One 8-ounce container (1 cup) plain yogurt

2 teaspoons pure maple syrup

2 tablespoons fresh lemon juice

1 tablespoon Dijon, Meaux, or another French
  mustard

½ teaspoon ground ginger

½ teaspoon ground cumin

⅓ teaspoon ground cinnamon

Pinch of cayenne pepper

Salt to taste

1 head red leaf lettuce, separated into leaves

1. To make the salad, in a medium-size saucepan, bring the water to a boil.
   Add the salt, couscous, and peas, return to a boil, and stir well while the
   water is boiling for 2 to 3 minutes. Remove the pan from the heat, cover,
   and let stand until all the liquid is absorbed, 15 to 20 minutes.

2. Put the couscous and peas in a deep salad bowl. Add the walnuts, pecans,
   raisins, onion, cucumbers, and mint and toss gently to mix well.

3. Whisk the dressing ingredients together in a measuring cup or small bowl
   until smooth. Pour over the salad and mix until everything is well coated.
   Refrigerate for a couple of hours.

4. Just before serving, arrange the lettuce leaves over a large platter and spread
   the couscous salad over the top. Serve immediately.

# DUTCHESS COUNTY CRISPY SALAD
# WITH BLUE CHEESE DRESSING

*This tasty salad is best served after an appetizing main course. It is a lovely preamble to dessert.*

MAKES 6 TO 8 SERVINGS

1 head green oak-leaf lettuce, separated into leaves

1 bunch arugula, stems trimmed off

1 medium-size Belgian endive, separated into leaves and cut in half lengthwise

1 medium-size red onion, thinly sliced

2 ripe but firm avocados, peeled, pitted, and cubed

2 teaspoons fresh lemon juice

$\frac{1}{2}$ cup French-Style Roquefort Dressing (page 242), prepared ahead of time

1. To make the salad, tear the lettuce into bite-size pieces and put in a large salad bowl. Add the arugula, endive, and onion and toss gently to mix.
2. Put the avocado cubes in a small bowl and sprinkle them with the lemon juice. Toss to coat, then add them to the salad bowl and toss gently.
3. Just before serving, pour the dressing over the salad and toss to coat. Serve immediately.

*A sensitive approach to food may extend sensitivity, almost without effort on our part, into other areas of our lives.*

Alan Hooker

# GREEN BEAN AND TOMATO SALAD

*This salad makes an especially good appetizer during the summer and fall months, when the beans and tomatoes can be freshly harvested. It is also a good accompaniment to cold fish or egg dishes.*

MAKES 6 SERVINGS

*Salad*

1/2 pound tender, very thin French string beans (*haricots verts*), ends trimmed off

Pinch of salt

2 teaspoons fresh lemon juice

6 plum tomatoes, seeded and coarsely chopped

1 medium-size red onion, finely chopped

Leaves from 1 bunch fresh Italian parsley or cilantro, finely chopped

3 tablespoons extra virgin olive oil

Pinch of freshly ground black pepper

*Dressing*

6 tablespoons extra virgin olive oil

3 tablespoons fresh lemon juice

Few drops of Tabasco sauce

Salt and freshly ground black pepper to taste

1. To make the salad, combine the string beans, salt, and lemon juice in a large saucepan of boiling water and cook until crisp-tender, 3 to 4 minutes maximum. Drain and rinse under cold running water, then drain again thoroughly and distribute them equally among 6 salad plates.

2. Put the chopped tomatoes in a deep bowl. Add the onion, parsley, olive oil, a pinch of salt, and the pepper, and combine well. Arrange the tomato mixture over the string beans at the center of each plate.

3. Whisk together the dressing ingredients in a measuring cup or small bowl until thickened. Pour only over the beans and serve immediately.

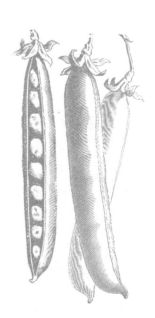

*October*

# CHILLED AMBER SALAD

*This salad is best served as an appetizer, especially during the late summer and early fall months.*

MAKES 6 TO 8 SERVINGS

## Salad

1 small head red cabbage

4 medium-size beets, cooked in boiling water to cover until tender, drained, peeled, and thinly sliced

1 medium-size red onion, thinly sliced

2 oranges, peeled, with white pith removed, and cut into eighths

1 cup pitted black olives, drained

## Dressing

5 tablespoons extra virgin olive oil

5 tablespoons hazelnut oil

5 tablespoons red wine vinegar

2 teaspoons honey

$1/2$ teaspoon Dijon mustard

Salt and freshly ground black pepper to taste

Chopped fresh dill or chervil for garnish

*What is not good for the hive is not good for the bees.*

Marcus Aurelius

1. To make the salad, cut the cabbage into quarters and cut out the core. Slice each quarter paper thin. Put the thinly shredded cabbage into a large salad bowl. Add the beets, onion, oranges, and olives and toss to mix well.
2. Whisk the dressing ingredients together in a measuring cup or small bowl until thickened. Pour over the salad and toss to coat evenly. Refrigerate for at least 1 hour.
3. Just before serving, divide the salad equally among 6 to 8 salad plates. Sprinkle with dill and serve immediately.

# COOKED FENNEL SALAD

*S*ince *fennel is a vegetable that helps one's digestion a great deal, this salad should be served after the main course.*

### Salad

2 fennel bulbs, stalks discarded

1 small head chicory, leaves cut in half

3 plum tomatoes, cut into wedges

2 scallions, finely chopped

1 small cucumber, peeled, seeded, and cubed

4 sprigs fresh Italian parsley, finely chopped

### Vinaigrette

$1/3$ cup extra virgin olive oil

$1/4$ cup balsamic vinegar

Salt and freshly ground black pepper to taste

1. To make the salad, cook the fennel bulbs in a medium-size saucepan of boiling salted water for 3 to 4 minutes. Drain and rinse under cold running water. Slice the bulbs and chill in the refrigerator for 1 hour.

2. Just before serving, put the fennel in a good-size salad bowl. Add the chicory, tomatoes, scallions, cucumber, and parsley and mix gently.

3. Whisk the vinaigrette ingredients together in a measuring cup or small bowl until thickened and drizzle over the salad. Toss lightly to coat and serve immediately.

*Earth is here so kind, that just tickle her with a hoe and she laughs with a harvest.*

Douglas Jerrold

# RED BEET SALAD
# WITH ROQUEFORT CHEESE

*This is an elegant appetizer any time of the year, but it is especially good in summer and fall, when the beets are fresh and in season.*

MAKES 4 TO 6 SERVINGS

### Salad

6 medium-size beets

2 green apples

1 teaspoon fresh lemon juice

1 bunch watercress, stems trimmed off

1 Belgian endive, separated into leaves and cut
  lengthwise into 1-inch-wide strips

### Dressing

$1/2$ cup low-fat sour cream

$1/2$ cup crumbled Roquefort cheese

2 shallots, coarsely chopped

3 tablespoons fresh lemon juice

2 tablespoons extra virgin olive oil

Salt and freshly ground black pepper to taste

Finely chopped fresh chives for garnish

1. To make the salad, cook the beets in a large saucepan of boiling salted water for 5 minutes. Drain, then rinse under cold running water and drain again. Peel and cut into matchsticks.

2. Peel, core, and cut the apples into matchsticks. Put them in a large salad bowl, toss with the lemon juice, add the beets, toss to combine, and refrigerate until ready to serve.

3. Combine the watercress and endive in a separate bowl.

4. Whisk the dressing ingredients together in a measuring cup or small bowl until it achieves a creamy consistency. Refrigerate until serving time.

5. When ready to serve, pour the dressing into the two bowls of vegetables and gently toss the salads until the vegetables are well coated with the dressing. Serve the beets and apples on one half of each salad plate and the watercress and endive on the other. Sprinkle with chives and serve immediately.

*Twelve Months of
Monastery Salads*

# RUSSIAN FRUIT AND VEGETABLE SALAD

MAKES 6 SERVINGS

4 large potatoes, peeled and cubed

2 medium-size carrots, peeled and cubed

1 cup frozen green peas

1 celery stalk, thinly sliced

1 dill or other pickle, cubed

2 medium-size apples, peeled, cored, and cubed

1 pear, peeled, cored, and cubed

2 scallions (white part only), finely chopped

3 tablespoons fresh lemon juice

2 teaspoons sugar

$\frac{1}{2}$ cup mayonnaise, homemade (page 238) or store-bought

1 head Boston lettuce

1. Cook separately in boiling salted water the potatoes (4 to 5 minutes), carrots (about 5 minutes), and peas (about 3 minutes), until each is tender. Drain and rinse each under cold running water. Put the drained vegetables in a deep salad bowl.

2. Add the celery, pickle, apples, pear, and scallions, pour the lemon juice over everything, and sprinkle evenly with the sugar. Toss gently to mix well. Spoon the mayonnaise over the salad and toss again to blend well.

3. Chill the salad for several hours. Just before serving, separate the lettuce into leaves and arrange them on a large serving platter. Place the salad on top and spread evenly over the lettuce. Serve cold.

*A man or a woman draws nearer to God as he or she withdraws further from the consolations of the world.*

Thomas à Kempis

# Avocado and Watercress Salad

*his salad is usually best served as an appetizer for lunch or brunch. It is particularly attractive when one harvests the shallots fresh from the garden.*

MAKES 4 SERVINGS

### Salad

4 small ripe but firm avocados, peeled, pitted, and
  sliced lengthwise

1 large bunch watercress, stems trimmed off

2 shallots, minced

6 small gherkins or cornichons, thinly sliced

### Vinaigrette

5 tablespoons hazelnut oil

3 tablespoons fresh lemon juice

Pinch of paprika

Salt and freshly ground black pepper to taste

1. Combine the salad ingredients in a large salad bowl.
2. Whisk together the vinaigrette ingredients in a measuring cup or small bowl until thickened. When ready to serve, pour it over the salad and gently toss a few times until everything is well coated. Serve immediately.

# CHERRY TOMATOES AND BULGUR SALAD

*This is an excellent salad to serve during the hot summer months or early in the fall season, when there is an abundance of tomatoes in the garden.*

1 cup bulgur

1 pound cherry tomatoes, cut in half

1 medium-size red onion, chopped

1 medium-size cucumber, peeled, seeded, and cubed

1/2 cup finely chopped fresh Italian parsley

1/4 cup finely chopped fresh mint

1/3 cup extra virgin olive oil

5 tablespoons fresh lemon juice

Salt and freshly ground black pepper to taste

1. Put the bulgur in a medium-size casserole and fill it halfway with cold water. Let the bulgur stand for several hours, until you are ready to use it. Just before preparing the salad, drain the bulgur in a strainer, rinse it under cold running water, and shake the strainer until no excess water remains.
2. Put the tomatoes, onion, and cucumber in a deep salad bowl.
3. In a separate bowl, mix together the drained bulgur, parsley, mint, olive oil, and lemon juice, season with salt and pepper, and toss well to combine. Add this to the salad bowl and toss to mix everything together well. You can refrigerate the salad for 1 hour and serve it cool in the summer, or serve it at room temperature during the fall months.

*Bad men live to eat and drink, whereas good men eat and drink in order to live.*

Socrates

# PENNE SALAD

*his salad may be served at room temperature, or refrigerated and served cold.*

### Salad

½ pound penne pasta

1 medium-size cucumber, peeled, cut in half
   lengthwise, seeded, and thinly sliced crosswise

1 medium-size red bell pepper, seeded and diced

12 pitted green olives

3 shallots, thinly sliced

2 sprigs fresh parsley, finely chopped

### Vinaigrette

3 tablespoons extra virgin olive oil

2 tablespoons red wine vinegar

Pinch of ground cumin

Salt and freshly ground black pepper to taste

1. Cook the penne in plenty of boiling salted water until *al dente*; do not overcook. Drain, then rinse under cold running water and drain again, shaking the colander well. Put the pasta in a large salad bowl and add the cucumber, red pepper, olives, and shallots. Just before serving, add the parsley.

2. Whisk together the vinaigrette ingredients in a measuring cup or small bowl. Taste and adjust the seasonings. Pour over the salad and toss gently to coat everything. Let the salad rest for 10 to 15 minutes, and then serve.

# RIGATONI AND BROCCOLI SALAD

## Salad

1 pound rigatoni, macaroni, or another pasta

1/2 pound broccoli, cut into florets

1 medium-size red bell pepper, seeded and diced

1/2 cup brine-cured black olives, drained and pitted

1/2 cup finely chopped scallions (white and tender green parts)

1/4 pound mozzarella cheese, cut into small pieces

## Vinaigrette

5 tablespoons extra virgin olive oil

2 teaspoons fresh lemon juice

2 teaspoons cider vinegar or vinegar of your choice

Pinch of dry mustard

Salt and freshly ground black pepper to taste

1. To make the salad, cook the rigatoni in a large saucepan of boiling salted water until *al dente*; do not overcook. Drain, then rinse under cold running water and drain again, shaking the colander well. Put the pasta in a large salad bowl.

2. While the pasta is cooking, steam the broccoli florets until crisp-tender, about 5 minutes. Drain and add to the salad bowl, along with the remaining salad ingredients.

3. Whisk together the vinaigrette ingredients in a measuring cup or small bowl until thickened. Taste and adjust the seasonings. Pour it over the salad and toss gently until everything is equally coated. Serve at room temperature or chill it and serve cold.

*Heaven is under our feet as well as over our heads.*

Henry David Thoreau

# ORECCHIETTE, ARUGULA, AND RADICCHIO SALAD

### MAKES 6 TO 8 SERVINGS

*Salad*

1 pound orecchiette pasta

1 bunch arugula, stems trimmed off

1 small head radicchio, separated into leaves and cut into thin ribbons

1 cup cherry tomatoes, cut in half

1 medium-size red onion, thinly sliced

⅓ cup niçoise olives or another olive of your choice, drained and pitted

*Vinaigrette*

3 tablespoons plus 1 teaspoon extra virgin olive oil

1 tablespoon plus 1 teaspoon balsamic vinegar

1 teaspoon fresh lemon juice

Salt and freshly ground black pepper to taste

1 cup freshly grated Parmesan cheese (optional)

1. Cook the orecchiette in a large saucepan of boiling salted water until *al dente*; do not overcook. Drain, then rinse under cold running water, and drain again, shaking the colander well. Put the pasta in a large salad bowl. Add the arugula, radicchio, tomatoes, onion, and the olives.

2. In a measuring cup or small bowl, whisk together the olive oil, vinegar, lemon juice, salt, and pepper until thickened. Just before serving, pour over the salad and toss until everything is coated. Add the Parmesan and blend some more. Serve at room temperature.

*The wise man does not seek through honors elevations;*
*Honor enough it is to be God's close relation.*

Angelus Silesius

# SALADE LANDAISE

*F*oie gras is a specialty from the Landes region in southwestern France, and traditionally, it is an integral part of this dish. To make this salad vegetarian, I have substituted cheese for the foie gras, but you can add some foie gras if you like.

**MAKES 6 SERVINGS**

### Salad

1½ pounds very thin French string beans *(haricots verts)*, ends trimmed off

1 cup croutons

3 shallots, minced

½ pound Swiss cheese or another cheese of your choice, diced

10 ounces cooked foie gras (optional), diced

### Vinaigrette

½ cup extra virgin olive oil

6 tablespoons tarragon vinegar

Salt and freshly ground black pepper to taste

Leaves from 1 bunch fresh tarragon, minced, for garnish

1. To make the salad, cook the string beans in a large saucepan of boiling salted water just until tender, 6 to 7 minutes. The beans must be tender yet firm. Drain, rinse them under cold running water, and shake the colander to drain them well. Put the beans in a salad bowl. Add the croutons, shallots, and cheese and toss gently. Right before serving, cover the top of the salad with the foie gras, if using.

2. Whisk the vinaigrette ingredients together in a measuring cup or small bowl until thickened and pour it evenly over the salad. Let it seep into the salad for a moment, sprinkle with the tarragon, and serve immediately.

# CARROT AND BLACK OLIVE SALAD
## (Carottes Rapées aux Olives)

his is a healthy and refreshing appetizer for a good meal any time of the year.

MAKES 6 TO 8 SERVINGS

*Salad*

12 medium-size carrots, peeled and cut into
   matchsticks

4 small shallots, minced

24 pitted black olives, cut in half

5 sprigs fresh Italian parsley, finely chopped

*Light Mayonnaise Dressing*

1 very fresh egg yolk

One 8-ounce container (1 cup) plain yogurt
   (low-fat is fine)

1 teaspoon Dijon, Meaux, or another French
   mustard

2 tablespoons fresh lemon juice

2 tablespoons extra virgin olive oil

Salt and freshly ground black pepper to taste

1. To assemble the salad, put the carrots, shallots, olives, and parsley in a
   good-size salad bowl. Toss to mix well.

2. Combine the dressing ingredients in a deep bowl. With an electric mixer,
   beat until the mayonnaise achieves a thick consistency. Pour over the salad
   and mix to coat everything thoroughly. Refrigerate and keep the salad cold
   up to several hours, until ready to be served.

*It was a common saying among the Puritans: "Brown bread and the
Gospel is good fare."*

Matthew Henry

# Potato Salad Holy Elder Simeon

*his is an excellent salad to serve cold or at room temperature as a side dish to salmon or another type of fish. Holy Simeon was the gracious elder from the Scriptures who was gifted to receive the Son of God in his arms.*

MAKES 6 TO 8 SERVINGS

*Salad*

1½ pounds boiling potatoes, cooked in boiling
water to cover until tender, drained, peeled, and
cubed
4 hard-boiled eggs, peeled and coarsely chopped
6 small ripe tomatoes, cored and quartered
1 small red onion, cut in half and sliced into
half-moons
½ cup pitted black olives, drained and cut in half
¼ cup capers, drained

*Vinaigrette*

⅓ cup extra virgin olive oil, or more if needed
¼ cup red wine vinegar, or more if needed
1 tablespoon Dijon mustard
Salt and freshly ground black pepper to taste

Leaves from 1 small bunch fresh chervil or curly
parsley, finely chopped, for garnish

1. To make the salad, put the potatoes, eggs, tomatoes, onion, olives, and capers in a large salad bowl.
2. Whisk together the vinaigrette ingredients in a measuring cup or small bowl until thickened, adding more oil and/or vinegar if needed. Just before serving, pour the dressing over the salad and toss gently until everything is well coated. Taste and adjust the seasonings, sprinkle with the chervil, and serve immediately.

# ST. FRANCIS SALAD

*S*t. Francis, the humble friar from Assisi, Italy, was a lover of God and all His creation. He was a gentle peacemaker, instilling in his followers the Gospel teachings of peace and nonviolence. His feast is celebrated on October 4.

MAKES 4 SERVINGS

## *Salad*

4 medium-size beets

6 medium-size potatoes, peeled

6 Belgian endives, separated into leaves

1 medium-size onion, finely chopped

## *Vinaigrette*

6 tablespoons extra virgin olive oil

2 teaspoons red or white wine vinegar

1 tablespoon Dijon, Meaux, or another French mustard

1 teaspoon salt

½ teaspoon freshly ground black pepper

Finely chopped fresh *fines herbes* mixture (tarragon, parsley, chervil, and chives) for garnish

1. To make the salad, bring the beets and potatoes to a boil in separate large saucepans filled with salted water, and continue to boil until tender when checked with a fork. Drain, rinse under cold running water, and drain again. Slip the skins off the beets, then cut both the beets and potatoes into long, thin slices, as one does for French fries. Put them in a salad bowl. Cut the endives lengthwise into thin strips and add to the salad bowl. Add the onion.

2. Whisk the vinaigrette ingredients together in a measuring cup or small bowl until thickened. Pour over the salad, sprinkle with the *fines herbes*, and toss lightly until everything is well coated. Serve immediately.

# RAINBOW SALAD

## Salad

2 sweet ripe melons, seeded and flesh cut from the rind and into chunks

1 cup seedless green grapes

2 red apples, peeled, cored, and cut into wedges

2 ripe but firm avocados, peeled, pitted, and cut into chunks

1 carrot, peeled and grated or finely shredded

2 tablespoons fresh lemon juice

$^1/_4$ pound sweet Gorgonzola cheese *(Gorgonzola dolce)*, crumbled

## Dressing

$^1/_3$ cup heavy cream, or more if needed

1 teaspoon dry mustard

1 teaspoon sugar

Pinch of salt

Pinch of white pepper

1. To assemble the salad, put the melons, grapes, apples, avocados, carrot, and lemon juice in a large salad bowl and toss to coat. Cover and refrigerate for at least 1 hour. Just before serving, add the crumbled Gorgonzola and mix gently.

2. Whisk the dressing ingredients together in a measuring cup or small bowl until smooth, then taste and adjust the seasonings. Pour over the salad, toss to coat well, and serve immediately.

*A salad is like a Spanish inn. It accepts everyone and everything it can hold.*

Marie-Therese Carreras

# TUTTI-FRUTTI SALAD

*hough it can be served as an appetizer, this salad is best as a dessert, especially on a warm Indian summer night, when the fruits taste particularly refreshing.*

MAKES 6 TO 8 SERVINGS

*Salad*

1 pineapple, peeled, cored, and cut into small
  chunks

1 ripe papaya, peeled, seeded, and diced

2 red apples, peeled, cored, and thinly sliced

8 fresh strawberries, hulled and cut in half

2 ripe but firm bananas, peeled and cut into rounds

*Dressing*

6 tablespoons orange juice

5 tablespoons fresh lemon juice

5 tablespoons honey

2 tablespoons dry sherry

$\frac{1}{2}$ teaspoon ground ginger

A few fresh mint leaves, finely chopped, for garnish

1. Combine the salad ingredients in a large glass bowl, mixing them together well. Cover and refrigerate for at least 2 hours before serving.

2. Put the dressing ingredients in a blender and whirl until smooth. When ready to serve, pour the dressing over the salad and toss to coat everything well. Garnish the top with the mint and serve immediately.

*The vegetable world presents no less variety to our nourishment, no fewer resources.*

Anthelme Brillat-Savarin

# PERSIMMON AND GREENS SALAD

### Salad

1 cup walnuts

1 bunch dandelion greens, stems trimmed off

1 bunch arugula, stems trimmed off

2 medium-size Belgian endives, separated into leaves

1 small head baby chicory (frisée)

1 small red onion, thinly sliced

2 persimmons, peeled and trimmed at both ends

$\frac{1}{3}$ cup crumbled blue cheese

### Dressing

$\frac{1}{4}$ cup half-and-half (optional)

$\frac{1}{3}$ cup extra virgin olive oil

3 tablespoons balsamic vinegar

Salt and freshly ground black pepper to taste

1. Preheat the oven to 350°F. Spread the walnuts on a cookie sheet and roast them in the oven until lightly browned, 6 to 8 minutes. Remove from the oven and set aside in a bowl to cool. Chop coarsely and set aside.

2. Gather the salad greens in a large salad bowl. Rip the frisée into small pieces. Add the onion.

3. Cut the persimmons into thin slices, then cut them into thin strips. Add them to the salad bowl. Add the crumbled cheese and walnuts and mix everything well.

4. Whisk the dressing ingredients together in a measuring cup or small bowl until thickened. Just prior to serving, pour over the salad. Taste and adjust the seasonings. Toss to coat everything evenly. Serve immediately.

Habit de Vinaigrié

# November

QUICK BELGIAN-STYLE SALAD 198

MEXICAN SALAD (*ENSALADA MÉJICANA*) 199

NEW YORK COLUMBIA COUNTY SALAD 200

MEDITERRANEAN LENTIL AND RICE SALAD 201

MONASTERY BEET RÉMOULADE 202

MACARONI AND GREEN BEAN SALAD 203

SMOKED SALMON AND APPLE APPETIZER 204

SALAD FROM THE AUVERGNE (*SALADE AUVERGNATE*) 205

*SALADE NIVERNAISE* 206

*SALADE POITEVINE* 207

*SALADE CAMPAGNARDE* 208

ST. ANDREW "THE FIRST CALLED" SALAD 209

ST. CECILE CAULIFLOWER SALAD 210

ST. MARTIN SALAD 211

PEAR AND WATERCRESS SALAD 212

# QUICK BELGIAN-STYLE SALAD

## Salad

1 firm, tart apple, left unpeeled, cut in half, cored,
   and thinly sliced

2 good-size Belgian endives, separated into leaves
   and cut in half lengthwise

1 bunch watercress, stems trimmed off

## Dressing

6 tablespoons extra virgin olive oil

3 tablespoons cider vinegar

2 tablespoons honey

1 teaspoon Dijon mustard

1 small shallot, minced

Salt and freshly ground black pepper to taste

¼ cup crumbled mild blue cheese for garnish

1. To make the salad, put the apple, endives, and watercress in a large salad
   bowl and toss to combine.
2. Whisk the dressing ingredients together in a measuring cup or small bowl
   until thickened. Just before serving, pour the dressing over the salad and
   toss with your hands until everything is evenly coated. Distribute the salad
   equally among 4 salad plates and sprinkle each portion with some of the
   crumbled cheese. Serve immediately.

# MEXICAN SALAD

## *(Ensalada Méjicana)*

MAKES 6 TO 8 SERVINGS

*Salad*

2 cups cooked long-grain white rice

2 carrots, peeled, cubed, cooked in boiling salted
water until tender, and drained

1 medium-size red onion, diced

One 8-ounce can corn kernels, drained and rinsed
under cold running water

1 yellow bell pepper, seeded and cut into long, thin
strips

1 medium-size gherkin, cubed

A few sprigs fresh cilantro, finely chopped

*Dressing*

⅓ cup extra virgin olive oil

5 tablespoons fresh lemon juice

Pinch of ground cumin

Salt and freshly ground black pepper to taste

1 head leafy lettuce of your choice, separated into
leaves

1. Combine the salad ingredients in a large salad bowl. Mix together lightly,
cover, and refrigerate for at least 2 hours.
2. Just before serving, whisk the dressing ingredients together in a measuring
cup or small bowl until thickened. Pour over the salad and stir to mix well.
Taste and adjust the seasonings. Serve the salad cold over a bed of lettuce.

*The most instructive experiences are those of everyday life.*

Friedrich
Nietzsche

# NEW YORK COLUMBIA COUNTY SALAD

*This simple salad is a good starter to an elegant, convivial meal. It can also be served after the main course.*

## Salad

4 medium-size beets, peeled and cubed

1 pound mixed salad greens

1 small red onion, finely chopped

$1/2$ cup pecans, coarsely chopped

$1/4$ pound Coach Farm or another goat cheese, crumbled

3 sprigs fresh Italian parsley, finely chopped

## Vinaigrette

$1/3$ cup extra virgin olive oil

$1/4$ cup balsamic vinegar

2 teaspoons Dijon mustard

Salt and freshly ground black pepper to taste

*Do what is good and seek peace in everything.*

St. John of the Cross

1. To make the salad, cook the beets in a large saucepan of boiling salted water until just tender, about 5 minutes. Drain, rinse under cold running water, drain again, and set aside.

2. Tear the greens into bite-size pieces and put in a large salad bowl. Add the beets and onion.

3. Toast the pecans in a dry skillet over medium heat, stirring, until they begin to give off a roasted scent, about 6 minutes, then add them to the salad. Add the cheese and parsley and mix well.

4. Whisk the vinaigrette ingredients together in a measuring cup or small bowl until thickened. Taste and adjust the seasonings. Just before serving, pour over the salad and toss to coat evenly. Serve immediately.

# MEDITERRANEAN LENTIL AND RICE SALAD

MAKES 6 TO 8 SERVINGS

*Salad*

2¹/₂ cups water

1 cup long-grain white rice

1 tablespoon olive oil

Sea salt

1 cup dried French lentils, picked over and rinsed

1 cup cherry tomatoes

1 medium-size cucumber, peeled, quartered
   lengthwise, seeded, and cubed

1 medium-size onion, finely chopped

¹/₂ cup pitted black olives, drained and coarsely
   chopped

*Dressing*

¹/₂ cup extra virgin olive oil

3 tablespoons red wine vinegar

2 tablespoons fresh lemon juice

1 teaspoon sugar

1 teaspoon Dijon mustard

¹/₂ teaspoon dried thyme

Salt and freshly ground black pepper to taste

¹/₂ cup crumbled feta cheese for garnish

1. Bring the water to a boil in a medium-size saucepan; add the rice, olive oil, and a dash of sea salt. Reduce the heat to medium-low, cover, and continue to cook until all the water is absorbed. When the rice is cooked, remove from the heat and allow to cool.

2. Meanwhile, fill a medium-size pan with water, bring to a boil over medium-high heat, add ¹/₄ teaspoon of sea salt, and cook the lentils until tender, about 20 minutes. Drain, rinse under cold running water, drain again, and put in a large salad bowl. Add the rice, cherry tomatoes, cucumber, onion, and olives and mix well.

3. Put the dressing ingredients in a blender and whirl until uniform in consistency. Taste and adjust the seasonings. Pour over the salad and toss to coat. Refrigerate the salad for 2 hours.

4. Just before serving, sprinkle the salad with the feta and serve immediately.

# MONASTERY BEET RÉMOULADE

### Salad

6 medium-size red beets, peeled and cut into matchsticks

1 small onion, cut into matchsticks

¼ cup fresh lemon juice

### Rémoulade Sauce

1 very fresh egg yolk

2 tablespoons Dijon, Meaux, or another French mustard

½ cup extra virgin olive oil

1 tablespoon tarragon vinegar

Salt and freshly ground black pepper to taste

Chopped fresh chervil or dill for garnish

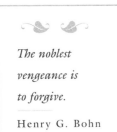

*The noblest vengeance is to forgive.*

Henry G. Bohn

1. To make the salad, cook the beets and onion in a large saucepan of boiling salted water for about 5 minutes, until tender. Drain, rinse under cold running water, then drain again thoroughly. Put the beets in a deep bowl, add the lemon juice, mix well, and refrigerate for several hours.

2. To make the sauce, put the egg yolk in another deep bowl and whisk in the mustard. Add the oil gradually, beating the mixture constantly with an electric mixer. Add the vinegar, season with salt and pepper, and continue to beat until the sauce achieves a uniform consistency. Refrigerate, covered, until ready to use.

3. When ready to serve, blend the beets and onion with the sauce until everything is well coated. Garnish the top with the chervil. Serve cold as an appetizer.

# MACARONI AND GREEN BEAN SALAD

MAKES 4 TO 6 SERVINGS

## Salad

³/4 pound macaroni

¹/2 pound string beans, ends trimmed off, and cut
in half

1 medium-size red onion, thinly sliced

12 small cherry tomatoes, cut in half

¹/2 cup brine-cured black olives, drained, pitted, and
chopped

A few fresh basil leaves, finely chopped

A few sprigs fresh Italian parsley, finely chopped

## Vinaigrette

5 tablespoons extra virgin olive oil

2 teaspoons tarragon or another vinegar of your
choice

1 teaspoon fresh lemon juice

Sea salt and freshly ground black pepper to taste

1. To make the salad, cook the macaroni in a large saucepan of boiling salted water until *al dente*. Drain and rinse under cold running water. Drain again, shaking the colander well, then transfer to a large salad bowl.

2. While the pasta is cooking, put the string beans in another large saucepan of boiling salted water and cook until tender but still crisp and firm, about 5 minutes. Drain and rinse under cold running water, then drain again. Add to the salad bowl, along with the onion, tomatoes, olives, and herbs.

3. Whisk the vinaigrette ingredients together in a measuring cup or small bowl until thickened. Pour over the salad and toss until the ingredients are well coated. Serve the salad at room temperature or refrigerate it for 1 hour and serve cold.

*There is a great deal of unmapped country within each of us.*

George Eliot

# SMOKED SALMON AND APPLE APPETIZER

*As the recipe name indicates, this salad should be served as an appetizer, at the beginning of the meal. Those who eat meat may wish to replace the salmon with slices of smoked ham or prosciutto di Parma, ham from Bayonne, France, or from Serrano, Spain. I occasionally substitute pears for the apples.*

MAKES 4 SERVINGS

## Salad

½ pound mâche or watercress, stems trimmed off

3 tart apples, peeled, cored, and thinly sliced

8 long strips smoked salmon

1 lemon

16 pecans, coarsely chopped, for garnish

## Dressing

7 tablespoons extra virgin olive oil

2 tablespoons fresh lemon juice

½ teaspoon Dijon mustard

Salt and freshly ground black pepper to taste

*We cannot fail in following nature.*

Montaigne

1. Put the mâche in a large salad bowl.
2. Divide the apple slices equally among 4 salad plates. Add 2 salmon strips to each plate. Cut the lemon and sprinkle some of its juice over the salmon and apples.
3. Toast the pecans in a small dry skillet over medium heat, stirring, until they begin to give off a roasted scent, 4 to 5 minutes. Remove from the skillet and set aside.
4. Whisk together the dressing ingredients in a measuring cup or small bowl until thickened. Taste and adjust the seasonings. Pour half of it over the mâche and toss to coat well. Arrange the greens so they cover one third of each salad plate. Pour the remaining dressing over the salmon and apples. Sprinkle everything with the toasted pecans. Serve immediately.

# SALAD FROM THE AUVERGNE

## (Salade Auvergnate)

*This salad is usually served at a family or friends' gathering. It can also be served as a main course for lunch or brunch.*

MAKES 4 TO 6 SERVINGS

### Salad

1 small head tender escarole, large leaves cut in half

4 hard-boiled eggs, peeled and quartered lengthwise

1/4 pound Bleu d'Auvergne or another blue cheese, crumbled

1/4 pound Cantal or Swiss cheese, diced

3/4 cup croutons

A few thin strips cured French ham from the Auvergne, prosciutto di Parma, or Serrano ham from Spain (optional)

### Vinaigrette

1/3 cup hazelnut oil or extra virgin olive oil

5 tablespoons tarragon vinegar

2 teaspoons Dijon, Meaux, or another French mustard

Salt and freshly ground black pepper to taste

1 bunch fresh chives, finely chopped, for garnish

1. Choose a large, flat oval platter to present this dish. To assemble the salad, distribute the escarole evenly over the whole platter. Arrange the egg slices around the outer edge, following the oval pattern of the platter. Crumble the blue cheese over the top of the escarole. Distribute the Cantal cheese and croutons evenly over the salad. If using, arrange the ham strips in a decorative fashion over the salad.

2. Combine the vinaigrette ingredients in a blender and whirl for a few seconds. Pour it evenly over the entire salad. Sprinkle the top with the chives and present the platter at the table.

# SALADE NIVERNAISE

*This salad is a meal in itself and as such is often served for a hasty lunch or brunch. It originated in the area of Burgundy called Nièvre, hence its name.*

MAKES 6 SERVINGS

### Salad

½ pound baby spinach

2 cups cauliflower florets, cooked in boiling salted water for 5 minutes and drained

1 small red onion, cut in half and thinly sliced into half-moons

2 hard-boiled eggs, peeled and coarsely chopped

1 Belgian endive, torn into bite-size pieces

1 cup diced ham (optional)

### Vinaigrette

⅓ cup extra virgin olive oil

3 tablespoons fresh lemon juice

1 tablespoon Dijon mustard

Dash of ground nutmeg

Salt and freshly ground black pepper to taste

1 small bunch fresh chives, finely chopped, for garnish

1. Combine the salad ingredients in a large salad bowl and toss gently to mix well.
2. Just before serving, whisk the vinaigrette ingredients together in a measuring cup or small bowl until thickened. Pour over the salad and toss lightly until everything is well coated. Sprinkle with the chives and serve immediately.

*What we give to the poor for Christ's sake is what we carry with us when we die.*

Peter Maurin

# SALADE POITEVINE

*This colorful and flavorful salad from the Poitou region of France is a lovely choice for a festive occasion.*

MAKES 4 TO 6 SERVINGS

*Vinaigrette*

²⁄₃ cup hazelnuts

¹⁄₃ cup extra virgin olive oil

3 tablespoons Raspberry-Scented Vinegar (page 236) or another vinegar of your choice

Salt and freshly ground black pepper to taste

*Salad*

1 pound baby spinach

1 medium-size red bell pepper, seeded and cut into small dice

1 medium-size yellow bell pepper, seeded and cut into small dice

2 shallots, minced

6 white mushrooms, thinly sliced

1. Preheat the oven to 300°F. Toast the nuts on a baking sheet until golden, 12 to 15 minutes. Remove from the oven, allow to cool, then rub them to remove the skins. Chop the nuts coarsely and put them in a measuring cup or small bowl. Add the remaining vinaigrette ingredients and stir to mix well. Let the vinaigrette stand until ready to use.

2. Put the salad ingredients in a large salad bowl and toss gently to mix. Just before serving, pour the vinaigrette over the salad and toss lightly to coat everything well. Serve at room temperature.

# SALADE CAMPAGNARDE

*This is a basic country-style salad, a peasant recipe, which could serve well for people who entertain weekend guests. Those who are not vegetarians may add diced ham or thin prosciutto strips and thus make this salad a complete meal.*

MAKES 6 TO 8 SERVINGS

### Salad

1 medium-size head broccoli, cut into bite-size florets

1 medium-size head cauliflower, cut into bite-size florets

6 white mushrooms, thinly sliced

2 tablespoons fresh lemon juice

16 cherry tomatoes

8 radishes, trimmed and thinly sliced

4 scallions, thinly sliced

1 cup cubed cheese of your choice (Swiss cheese is nice)

### Vinaigrette

$\frac{1}{2}$ cup extra virgin olive oil

$\frac{1}{4}$ cup Spanish sherry vinegar (preferably Jerez)

1 tablespoon Worcestershire sauce

1 garlic clove, minced

Salt and freshly ground black pepper to taste

1. To make the salad, cook the broccoli and cauliflower florets in the top of a double boiler, covered, over simmering water until tender, about 15 minutes. Or cook them in a large saucepan of boiling salted water for about 5 minutes. Pat dry with paper towels, allow to cool, and transfer to a good-size salad bowl.

2. In a small bowl, mix the mushroom slices with the lemon juice, then add them to the salad bowl. Add the cherry tomatoes, radishes, and scallions and toss gently to mix. Just before serving, add the cheese.

3. Whisk the vinaigrette ingredients together in a measuring cup or small bowl until thickened and, at the last minute, pour over the salad. Toss to coat everything well. Serve immediately.

# St. Andrew
# "The First Called" Salad

*S*t. Andrew, the brother of St. Peter, was the first disciple called by Christ. His feast is celebrated on November 30. This salad is always served as an appetizer, though it could also be served as the main course for lunch or brunch.

**MAKES 4 SERVINGS**

## Salad

1 large bunch spinach, trimmed of heavy stems

One 3.5-ounce can tuna, drained and coarsely
    chopped

8 white mushrooms, thinly sliced

1 medium-size to large ripe but firm avocado,
    peeled, pitted, and sliced

## French Deluxe Dressing

$\frac{1}{3}$ cup extra virgin olive oil

$\frac{1}{4}$ cup fresh lemon juice

1 tablespoon prepared chili sauce

1 teaspoon Dijon mustard

1 teaspoon prepared horseradish

1 garlic clove, minced

$\frac{1}{2}$ teaspoon paprika

Salt and freshly ground black pepper to taste

1 hard-boiled egg, peeled and coarsely chopped, for
garnish

1. To assemble the salad, put the spinach in a large salad bowl. Add the tuna, mushrooms, and avocado and toss gently to mix.

2. Whirl the dressing ingredients together in a blender, then pour over the salad. Mix until everything is well coated. Sprinkle with the chopped egg and serve immediately.

*Taste the feast by nature spread.*

Samuel Johnson

# St. Cecile Cauliflower Salad

*t. Cecile, or Cecilia, was a famous Roman noblewoman who suffered martyrdom for confessing her fidelity to Christ. She is the patron saint of musicians, and her feast is celebrated on November 22. Serve this salad as an appetizer during the harvest months, when the tomatoes are ripe and at their best.*

MAKES 4 TO 6 SERVINGS

### Salad

1 large or 2 medium-size heads cauliflower

6 medium-size ripe tomatoes, peeled and diced

1 medium-size red onion, cut in half and thinly sliced into half-moons

### Vinaigrette

$1/4$ cup extra virgin olive oil

3 tablespoons walnut oil

3 tablespoons fresh lemon juice

Salt and freshly ground black pepper to taste

1 head Boston lettuce, separated into leaves

1. To make the salad, put the cauliflower in a container filled with cold water for at least 1 hour, or until ready to use. Carefully separate the florets and slice the top parts of the stem (the good ones) into thin slices. Discard the tough parts. Put the cauliflower in a saucepan. Add water to cover and salt to taste, bring to a boil over medium heat, and continue to boil until tender, 6 to 7 minutes. Drain immediately after and rinse under cold running water so as to preserve freshness and color. Or cook the cauliflower in the top of a double boiler, covered, over simmering water for about 15 minutes, and rinse with cold water. Drain and set aside.

2. Just prior to serving, mix together the cauliflower, tomatoes, and onion in a deep bowl.

3. Whisk together the vinaigrette ingredients in a measuring cup or small bowl until thickened and pour over the vegetables. Toss the salad with care and make sure that all vegetables are well coated. Set 3 or 4 lettuce leaves on each salad plate and arrange the salad evenly on top. Serve immediately.

# St. Martin Salad

*S*t. Martin of Tours was inspired by the life and example of St. Anthony, the father of monks. He embraced the monastic life in the solitude of Ligugé, near Poitiers. Later on, as Bishop of Tours, he continued to promote monastic life in his diocese and throughout France. He is one of the most popular saints of France and his feast is celebrated on November 11.

**MAKES 4 SERVINGS**

*Salad*

1 large ripe but firm avocado

2 Belgian endives, separated into leaves

1 bunch watercress, stems trimmed off

1 large carrot, peeled and very finely grated or
    shredded

½ cup thinly sliced mushrooms (optional)

*Vinaigrette*

6 tablespoons extra virgin olive oil

2 tablespoons wine vinegar (preferably tarragon-
    flavored white wine vinegar)

Dash of dry mustard

Salt and freshly ground black pepper to taste

1. To assemble the salad, peel the avocado, remove the pit, and cut into chunks. Put it in a large salad bowl, along with the endives, watercress, carrot, and mushrooms, if using.

2. Whisk together the vinaigrette ingredients in measuring cup or small bowl until thickened. Pour over the salad just before serving and toss lightly to coat everything. Serve immediately.

*There is no stopping place in this life—no, nor is there ever one for any man, no matter how far along his way he's gone.*

Meister Eckehart

# PEAR AND WATERCRESS SALAD

## Salad

1 cup pecan halves

1 large bunch watercress, stems trimmed off

3 firm pears, peeled, cored, and sliced lengthwise

1 small head baby chicory (frisée), torn into small
pieces

$^1/_2$ cup crumbled Gorgonzola or another blue
cheese

## Dressing

$^1/_3$ cup extra virgin olive oil, or more if needed

4 teaspoons fresh lemon juice

$^1/_2$ teaspoon ground ginger or peeled and grated
fresh ginger

Salt and freshly ground black pepper to taste

1. Preheat the oven to 350°F. To make the salad, spread the pecans on a
baking sheet and toast until lightly browned and fragrant, 6 to 8 minutes.
Remove from the oven and set aside to cool.
2. In a large salad bowl, combine the watercress, pears, frisée, the cooled
pecans, and the cheese. Mix together gently.
3. Whisk together the dressing ingredients in a measuring cup or small bowl.
Pour over the salad, toss to coat, and serve immediately.

*Humanity is milk, wine the divinity,*
*If you drink milk and wine, you'll greatly strengthened be.*

Angelus Silesius

# DECEMBER

MUSHROOM SALAD, GREEK STYLE    214

HERBED TOFU SALAD    215

ROOM-TEMPERATURE RED SALAD    216

ROASTED ONION SALAD    217

SOUTH AMERICAN BEAN SALAD
(*ENSALADA SUDAMERICANA*)    218

INDIAN CURRIED LENTIL SALAD    219

ROASTED SWEET PEPPER SALAD FROM THE PIEDMONT
(*INSALATA PIEDMONTESE*)    220

ARTICHOKE HEART SALAD (*INSALATA DI CARCIOFI*)    221

MONASTERY-STYLE COLESLAW    222

*SALADE NANTAISE*    223

IMMACULATA SALAD    224

STUFFED AVOCADO SALAD    225

CLEMENTINE, APPLE, AND SPINACH SALAD    226

ORANGE, APPLE, AND FENNEL SALAD    227

ORANGE AND AVOCADO SALAD    228

# MUSHROOM SALAD, GREEK STYLE

½ cup extra virgin Greek or another olive oil

¼ cup white wine vinegar

2 tablespoons tomato paste

1 pound small white mushrooms

16 small white onions, peeled and left whole

1 fennel bulb, stalks discarded, bulb quartered, then
sliced lengthwise paper thin

½ teaspoon dried oregano

½ teaspoon dried thyme

½ teaspoon garlic powder

Salt and freshly ground black pepper to taste

1. Pour the olive oil into a large saucepan. Add the vinegar and tomato paste
   and stir, over medium-low heat, until dissolved.
2. Add the mushrooms, onions, and fennel to the hot dressing and stir
   constantly. Add the oregano, thyme, and garlic and season with salt and
   pepper. Reduce the heat to low and continue to cook for another 12 to 15
   minutes, until the vegetables are tender. Stir occasionally so as to not let the
   mixture burn on the bottom.
3. Remove from the heat and allow it to cool. Transfer the mixture to a salad
   bowl and refrigerate for at least 3 hours before serving. Serve cold.

*I eat to live, to serve and also, it happens, to enjoy, but I do not eat
for the sake of enjoyment.*

Mahatma Gandhi

# HERBED TOFU SALAD

*This is a light and nutritious salad that can be served as an appetizer or after the main course.*

MAKES 8 SERVINGS

*Salad*

1 small head Boston lettuce, torn into bite-size
   pieces

1 small Belgian endive, torn into bite-size pieces

1 cup assorted chopped fresh herbs: chives, parsley,
   chervil, dill, and/or mint

One 10-ounce package firm tofu, drained, rinsed,
   patted dry, and cut into small cubes or crumbled

2 shallots, minced

*Dressing*

6 tablespoons extra virgin olive oil

6 tablespoons walnut oil

1/4 cup Spanish sherry vinegar (preferably Jerez)

1 teaspoon fresh lemon juice

Salt and freshly ground black pepper to taste

1. To assemble the salad, combine the lettuce, endive, and herbs in a large
   salad bowl. Add the tofu cubes and shallots and toss gently to combine.

2. Just before serving, whisk the dressing ingredients together in a measuring
   cup or small bowl until thickened. Taste and adjust the seasonings. Pour
   over the salad and toss to coat everything evenly. Serve immediately.

*December*

215

# ROOM-TEMPERATURE RED SALAD

*T*his salad is recommended as a refreshing palate cleanser after the main course and before an enticing dessert.

MAKES 6 TO 8 SERVINGS

*Salad*

1 head red oak-leaf lettuce

1 small head radicchio, torn into bite-size pieces

1/2 small head red cabbage, cored and thinly shredded

1 medium-size red onion, cut in half and thinly sliced into half-moons

3 tangerines or clementines, peeled, with white pith removed, and separated into segments

1 small red bell pepper, seeded and cut into long, thin strips

*Dressing*

1/4 cup walnut oil

3 tablespoons extra virgin olive oil

3 tablespoons red wine vinegar

Pinch of dry mustard

Pinch of sugar

Salt and freshly ground black pepper to taste

1. To assemble the salad, put the lettuce in a large salad bowl. Add the radicchio, cabbage, onion, tangerines, and bell pepper and toss together gently.

2. Just before serving, whisk the dressing ingredients together in a measuring cup or small bowl until thickened. Drizzle it over the salad and toss lightly until everything is well coated. Serve immediately.

# ROASTED ONION SALAD

*his is an intriguing and original appetizer that should be served only to guests who love onions. You can also serve it as an accompaniment to fish or poultry. If you like, add cherry tomato slices and a few olives to each serving for extra color.*

**MAKES 4 TO 6 SERVINGS**

*Salad*

1 pound medium-size sweet onions (Vidalias are ideal)

*Vinaigrette*

1/2 cup olive oil

1/4 cup Spanish sherry vinegar (preferably Jerez) or another vinegar of your choice

1 tablespoon Dijon, Meaux, or another French mustard

1 head Boston lettuce or another lettuce of your choice

1. Preheat the oven to 350°F. Put the onions whole, and without peeling them, on a baking sheet and bake in the oven for 30 minutes. Take them out and allow to cool. With the help of a small pointed knife, peel the onions carefully so that they remain intact. When they are all peeled, carefully cut them in half lengthwise.
2. Whisk the vinaigrette ingredients together in a measuring cup or small bowl until thickened.
3. On each individual plate, put 3 lettuce leaves and top with 3 or 4 onion halves. Pour the vinaigrette over them and serve.

*A man there was and they called him mad, the more he gave the more he had.*

John Bunyan

*December*

# SOUTH AMERICAN BEAN SALAD

## *(Ensalada Sudamericana)*

MAKES 6 SERVINGS

### *Salad*

5 medium-size red potatoes, peeled and cubed

3 cups freshly cooked or canned small or medium-size white navy beans, drained and rinsed

6 gherkins or cornichons, thinly sliced

1 medium-size white onion, chopped

1 medium red bell pepper, seeded and diced

### *Vinaigrette*

1/2 cup extra virgin olive oil

1/4 cup red wine vinegar

Pinch of paprika

Salt and freshly ground black pepper to taste

2 hard-boiled eggs, peeled and coarsely chopped, for garnish

1. To make the salad, cook the potatoes in boiling salted water just until tender, drain, and rinse under cold running water. Put in a large salad bowl, add the remaining salad ingredients, and refrigerate for at least 2 hours.

2. Just before serving, whisk the vinaigrette ingredients together in a measuring cup or small bowl until thickened. Pour over the salad and gently toss until all the ingredients are thoroughly coated. Sprinkle the chopped eggs on top and serve immediately.

*The trouble is, people do not work in peace and quiet. They bustle, like Martha.*

Dorothy Day

# INDIAN CURRIED LENTIL SALAD

*This recipe may not be for everyone, but it is certainly appetizing to those who love Indian spices.*

## Salad

2 cups dried small lentils (the crunchy French lentils are best)

1 long, thin cucumber, peeled, seeded, and cubed

2 celery stalks, sliced in half lengthwise, then thinly sliced crosswise

1 medium-size onion, finely chopped

## Dressing

6 tablespoons vegetable or extra virgin olive oil

3 tablespoons fresh lemon juice

1 garlic clove, minced

2 teaspoons curry powder

$1/2$ teaspoon ground cumin

$1/3$ teaspoon chili powder

Salt and freshly ground black pepper to taste

Chopped fresh cilantro for garnish

1. To make the salad, in a large saucepan of salted water, bring the lentils to a boil. Reduce the heat to medium and simmer until tender, about 30 minutes. Drain, then rinse under cold running water. Shake the colander well and put the lentils in a large salad bowl. Add the cucumber, celery, and onion and stir to mix well.

2. Whisk the dressing ingredients together in a measuring cup or small bowl until thickened and the spices are dissolved. Taste and adjust the seasonings. Pour over the lentil mixture and blend thoroughly. Cover the salad and refrigerate for several hours.

3. Just before serving, garnish the top with cilantro.

# ROASTED SWEET PEPPER SALAD
# FROM THE PIEDMONT

## (Insalata Piedmontese)

*This salad is always served as an appetizer, either for lunch or supper.*

**MAKES 4 TO 6 SERVINGS**

*Salad*

3 large red bell peppers

3 large yellow bell peppers

2 shallots, coarsely chopped

12 pitted green olives, sliced

1 cup diced fontina cheese

1/4 cup capers, drained

Handful chopped fresh Italian parsley

*Dressing*

1/2 cup plus 2 tablespoons extra virgin olive oil

2 tablespoons red wine vinegar

2 tablespoons fresh lemon juice

1 teaspoon Dijon, Meaux, or another French mustard

2 tablespoons honey

Salt and freshly ground black pepper to taste

1. Preheat the oven to 400°F or preheat the broiler. To make the salad, roast or broil the peppers, turning them as they turn black. Remove them when the skins are blackened all the way around and place in a brown paper bag until they cool off. Peel off their skins, then wash under cold running water to remove any remaining blackened bits. Pat dry with paper towels. Remove their stems, cut them in half, remove the seeds, slice into thin strips, and put in a salad bowl. Add the shallots, olives, cheese, capers, and parsley and toss to mix well.

2. Just before serving, combine the dressing ingredients in a blender and whirl for a few seconds until smooth. Pour the dressing over the salad and toss lightly until everything is coated well. Divide the salad among 4 to 6 salad plates and serve at room temperature.

# ARTICHOKE HEART SALAD

## (Insalata di Carciofi)

*This salad may be served as an attractive appetizer to an elegant dinner.*

**MAKES 6 SERVINGS**

*Salad*

6 medium-size artichokes

Pinch of salt

3 tablespoons fresh lemon juice

1 medium-size head radicchio, cut into thin strips

*Dressing*

1/2 cup extra virgin olive oil

6 tablespoons fresh lemon juice

1 garlic clove, minced

Salt and freshly ground black pepper to taste

A few sprigs fresh Italian parsley, finely chopped, for garnish

6 hard-boiled eggs, peeled and cut in half lengthwise

1. To prepare the artichokes, break off the leaves at the bottom and put each artichoke on its side on a cutting board. Using a sharp knife, cut the lower leaves off up to where the heart of the artichoke is found. Proceed to trim and cut off the leaves above the heart of the artichoke. Cut off and trim the rest of the leaves, following the same procedure, being careful to keep the heart intact. Using the knife or a spoon, scoop out and discard the choke. As you finish each one, put it in a medium-size saucepan filled with water to which you've added the salt and lemon juice. When you've finished, bring the water to a boil, reduce the heat to medium, and cook until tender, 12 to 15 minutes. Drain and allow to cool, then combine the cooled artichokes and the radicchio in a large salad bowl and mix together carefully.

2. Whisk the dressing ingredients together in a measuring cup or small bowl until thickened. Pour half of it over the vegetables and toss gently to coat. Divide the salad equally among 6 salad plates. Place 2 egg halves on each plate and sprinkle with the chopped parsley. Pour the remaining dressing over the egg halves and serve immediately.

*The beginnings of all things are small.*

Cicero

# MONASTERY-STYLE COLESLAW

*his basic coleslaw is nutritious and an excellent dish to serve any time of the year. It makes a good accompaniment to almost anything.*

**MAKES 6 TO 8 SERVINGS**

1 medium-size head green cabbage, cored and shredded

5 medium-size carrots, peeled and finely shredded

1 medium-size Vidalia onion, thinly sliced

½ cup mayonnaise, homemade (page 238) or store-bought

2 tablespoons distilled or white wine vinegar

2 tablespoons fresh lemon juice

Dash of salt and freshly ground black pepper to taste

½ cup golden raisins (optional)

1. Combine the cabbage, carrots, and onion in a large salad bowl. Add the remaining ingredients and mix together very well.
2. Cover and refrigerate for at least 2 hours prior to serving. Serve cold.

# SALADE NANTAISE

*his salad, from the region around Nantes in France, is usually served as an appetizer.*

### Salad

6 red potatoes, peeled

$\frac{1}{2}$ pound mâche or baby spinach

3 hard-boiled eggs, peeled and cut into rounds

### Vinaigrette

6 tablespoons hazelnut oil

3 tablespoons red wine vinegar

1 tablespoon Dijon, Meaux, or another French mustard

2 small shallots, minced

Salt and freshly ground black pepper to taste

1. To make the salad, cook the potatoes in a large saucepan of boiling salted water until tender, 15 to 20 minutes. The potatoes must remain firm, so don't let them cook until they're so soft they fall apart. Drain, rinse under cold running water, then pat dry. Allow the potatoes to cool completely, then slice them carefully into rounds. Put them in a salad bowl. Just before serving, add the mâche and sliced eggs.

2. Whisk the vinaigrette ingredients together in a measuring cup or small bowl until thickened. Pour over the salad and toss gently, trying to keep the egg slices intact. Serve immediately.

*Joy and sorrow are next-door neighbors.*

German proverb

# IMMACULATA SALAD

*he feast of the Immaculate Conception of Mary, the Mother of God, is celebrated on December 8. She is often referred to by the Latin name Immaculata. This salad is best served after the main course as a smooth transitional dish before dessert.*

**MAKES 6 TO 8 SERVINGS**

### Salad

1 head Boston lettuce, separated into leaves

1 bunch arugula, stems trimmed off

2 large green apples, peeled, cored, and sliced

$\frac{1}{3}$ cup whole almonds, toasted in a preheated 350°F oven until fragrant

$\frac{1}{2}$ cup crumbled Stilton or another blue cheese

### Dressing

$\frac{1}{3}$ cup hazelnut oil

5 tablespoons extra virgin olive oil

6 tablespoons tarragon or red wine vinegar

2 shallots, minced

2 tablespoons honey

1 teaspoon Dijon mustard

Salt and freshly ground black pepper to taste

1. To assemble the salad, put the lettuce, arugula, apples, toasted almonds, and crumbled cheese in a large salad bowl and toss together lightly.

2. Combine all the dressing ingredients in a blender and whirl for a few seconds until smooth. Just before serving, pour the dressing over the salad and toss gently to coat everything. Serve immediately.

*God's love means me alone, it is for me He burns,*
*He dies of sheer dismay if I for him not yearn.*

Angelus Silesius

# STUFFED AVOCADO SALAD

*his dish is usually served as an appetizer, but it can also be a main course for lunch or brunch.*

*Avocados*

2 large ripe but firm avocados

Fresh lemon juice as needed

*Stuffing*

2 tablespoons half-and-half

1/4 pound goat cheese, crumbled

1 tablespoon fresh lemon juice

2 tablespoons blanched almonds, coarsely chopped

2 tablespoons finely chopped fresh chives

3 tablespoons finely chopped fresh cilantro or
   Italian parsley

4 pitted black olives, finely chopped

Pinch of salt (optional)

White pepper to taste

1 head Boston lettuce, separated into leaves

1. Cut the avocados in half lengthwise. Remove the pits and gently peel. Scoop out 1 tablespoon of pulp from each half to make more room in the cavity for the stuffing. Drizzle all over with lemon juice to prevent the avocado from darkening.

2. To make the stuffing, pour the half-and-half in a small bowl and gradually add the goat cheese, mashing it into the half-and-half with a fork. Add the lemon juice, almonds, herbs, olives, salt (if needed), and pepper. Mix well and fill the centers of the avocado cavities equally with the mixture.

3. Place a few lettuce leaves on each salad plate and put a stuffed avocado half on top. Serve immediately.

# CLEMENTINE, APPLE, AND SPINACH SALAD

*Salad*

1 pound spinach, trimmed of heavy stems

4 clementines, peeled, with white pith removed, and
separated into segments

2 medium-size green apples, peeled, cored, and
sliced

8 radishes, trimmed and thinly sliced

1 medium-size red onion, thinly sliced

*Dressing*

⅓ cup heavy cream

¼ cup extra virgin olive oil

2 tablespoons white wine vinegar

1 teaspoon fresh lemon juice

1 teaspoon Dijon mustard

Salt and freshly ground black pepper to taste

3 hard-boiled eggs, peeled and coarsely chopped, for
garnish

1. To assemble the salad, combine the spinach, clementines, apples, radishes,
and onion in a large salad bowl and mix together well. Cover the bowl with
a clean towel and refrigerate until ready to use, at least 1 hour.

2. Combine the dressing ingredients in a blender and whirl until smooth.
When ready to serve, pour over the salad and toss to coat. Distribute the
salad among 6 or 8 salad plates. Sprinkle each serving with the chopped
eggs and serve immediately.

# Orange, Apple, and Fennel Salad

### Makes 6 servings

**Salad**

2 fennel bulbs, stalks discarded

2 medium-size oranges, peeled, with white pith
  removed, and separated into segments

2 green apples, peeled, cored, and sliced

**Dressing**

1/3 cup extra virgin olive oil

4 teaspoons fresh lemon juice

Salt and freshly ground black pepper to taste

6 dates, pitted and coarsely chopped, for garnish

1. To make the salad, cut the fennel in half and thinly slice. Put in a large salad bowl. Dice the oranges or cut each segment in half. Add to the salad bowl along with the apples and mix well. Cover and refrigerate for at least 2 hours before serving.

2. Whisk the dressing ingredients together in a measuring cup or small bowl until thickened. Just prior to serving, pour over the salad. Taste and adjust the seasonings. Toss to coat everything evenly. Sprinkle the dates over the top and serve while the salad is still chilled.

*The very best and utmost of attainment in this life is to remain still and let God act and speak in thee.*

Meister Eckehart

# ORANGE AND AVOCADO SALAD

*This salad is best served as an appetizer. It is a refreshing introduction to an elegant dinner.*

**MAKES 6 TO 8 SERVINGS**

### Dressing

1/2 cup hazelnut oil

1/4 cup fresh lime or lemon juice

2 teaspoons Tabasco sauce

Salt and freshly ground black pepper to taste

### Salad

3 oranges, peeled, with white pith removed, separated into segments, and cut in half

2 large ripe but firm avocados

2 Belgian endives, separated into leaves

2 scallions (white part only), thinly sliced

Leaves from 1 bunch fresh cilantro, finely chopped, for garnish

1. Whisk the dressing ingredients together in a large salad bowl.
2. To make the salad, add the oranges to the dressing and marinate in the refrigerator for at least 2 hours before serving.
3. Just before serving, cut the avocados in half, remove the peel and pit, and cut into cubes. Add the avocados, endives, and scallions to the salad bowl and toss to coat with the dressing. Sprinkle the cilantro on top and serve immediately.

*Overindulgence must be avoided in the monastery and a monk must never be overtaken by indigestion.*

St. Benedict

# SALAD OILS, VINEGARS, AND DRESSINGS

The French say, "a good salad starts with a good dressing." Vinaigrettes, and salad dressings in general, are meant to enhance both the taste and the presentation of the salad. They also go a long way to help achieve a perfect result: a dramatic, memorable salad that shall not be soon forgotten.

Basic salad dressings and sauces tend to be few in number, but they lend themselves to infinite variations. Take the basic French vinaigrette, which is made of good olive oil and wine vinegar *(le mariage de l'huile et du vinaigre)*, to which is added a pinch of salt and pepper to taste. This same vinaigrette offers endless possibilities the moment one starts adding other ingredients, be it a minced garlic clove, a teaspoon of Dijon mustard, a handful of finely chopped fresh herbs, or a combination of honey and mustard. The same can be said of the *sauce mayonnaise:* add a few minced garlic cloves and you have a *sauce aioli;* add extra Dijon or Meaux mustard and you create a *sauce rémoulade.* The field of vinaigrettes, dressings, and sauces is an open one, where any creative chef can always reinvent the recipe to give a magic touch to his salad.

Lots of varieties of vinaigrettes, dressings, and sauces are sold commercially. Though these simplify the task of the cook, they cannot in any way compare to the wonders of a homemade dressing or vinaigrette. Commercial dressings should be relegated to emergency use only, such as feeding a large crowd.

When you assemble the ingredients for a good dressing or vinaigrette, always start with the best: high-quality olive oil, a refined type of vinegar, sea salt, and freshly ground pepper. Additional ingredients should also be fresh: good tart lemons, fresh eggs for mayonnaise, and fresh herbs when required or good-quality dried ones when fresh are not available.

Any dressing, sauce, or vinaigrette can be prepared ahead of time and then refrigerated. It can be mixed in a blender or simply whisked by hand in a deep bowl. There is nothing mysterious about a good dressing or sauce: All the chef needs is plenty of creativity and ingenuity to transform an economical salad into gourmet fare. Many vinaigrettes, dressings, and sauces are already contained within the recipes themselves. What follows here are the basic and most used ones, which can serve as the inspiration for other varieties.

HERB-SCENTED OIL 232

SPICY OIL 233

CITRUS-SCENTED OIL 233

BASIL-SCENTED VINEGAR 234

LEMON VERBENA–SCENTED VINEGAR 234

SPICY BALSAMIC VINEGAR 235

RASPBERRY-SCENTED VINEGAR 236

SIMPLE VINAIGRETTE (*VINAIGRETTE CLASSIQUE*) 237

SPICY SPANISH VINAIGRETTE 238

MAYONNAISE 238

AIOLI MAYONNAISE 239

BLUE CHEESE DRESSING 239

THOUSAND ISLAND DRESSING 240

HONEY MUSTARD DRESSING 240

CREAMY MUSTARD DRESSING 241

FRENCH-STYLE HERB DRESSING 241

FRENCH-STYLE CREAMY LEMON DRESSING 242

FRENCH-STYLE ROQUEFORT DRESSING 242

TARRAGON SAUCE "CLASSIQUE" (*SAUCE À L'ESTRAGON*) 243

FESTIVE DRESSING 243

HONEY LEMON DRESSING 244

SPICY NAPOLEON SAUCE 244

# AROMATIC OR FLAVORED OILS AND VINEGARS

These oils and vinegars can add a dramatic touch to any salad—they're pure magic.

## HERB-SCENTED OIL

### MAKES 3 1/2 CUPS

| | |
|---|---|
| 3 cups olive oil | 1 sprig fresh rosemary |
| 2 shallots, minced | 3 sprigs fresh thyme |
| 2 bay leaves | 1 sprig fresh basil |

1. Pour the oil into a deep pot over medium-low heat. Add the remaining ingredients and cook for 3 to 4 minutes until fragrant. Turn off the heat and allow the oil to cool.

2. Pour the cooled oil through a fine-mesh strainer into a very clean bottle and discard the solids. Store it in a cool, dark place or refrigerate.

*When I have eaten the morsel on Wednesday, I do not look for it on Thursday.*

Russian proverb

# SPICY OIL

MAKES 2 1/2 CUPS

2½ cups sesame oil

3 jalapeños, seeded and minced

1 small onion, minced

3 garlic cloves, minced

1. Pour the oil into a deep pot over medium-low heat. Add the remaining ingredients and heat for 3 to 4 minutes until fragrant. Turn off the heat and allow the oil to cool.
2. Pour the cooled oil through a fine-mesh strainer into a very clean bottle and discard the solids. Store it in a cool, dark place or refrigerate.

# CITRUS-SCENTED OIL

MAKES 2 1/2 CUPS

2½ cups olive oil

1 long strip lemon peel, crushed

1 long strip lime peel, crushed

1 long strip orange peel, crushed

½ teaspoon fresh lemon juice

3 or 4 black peppercorns

1. Pour the oil into a deep pot over medium-low heat. Add the remaining ingredients and heat for 3 to 4 minutes, until fragrant. Stir well. Turn off the heat and allow the oil to cool.
2. Pour the cooled oil through a fine-mesh strainer into a very clean bottle and discard the solids. Store it in a cool, dark place or refrigerate.

# BASIL-SCENTED VINEGAR

*This vinegar is particularly good on a tomato salad.*

MAKES 3 CUPS

3 cups red wine vinegar

3 garlic cloves, minced

1 cup packed fresh basil leaves, finely chopped

1. Bring the vinegar to a boil in a deep pot over medium heat and let it continue to boil for 3 to 4 minutes. Turn off the heat and immediately add the garlic and basil. Cover the pot and allow the vinegar to cool for at least 2 hours.
2. When the vinegar has cooled, pour it through a fine-mesh strainer into a very clean bottle and discard the solids. Store it in a cool, dark place or refrigerate.

# LEMON VERBENA-SCENTED VINEGAR

*This vinegar is excellent on green salads and seafood salads.*

MAKES 3 CUPS

3 cups cider vinegar

1 cup finely chopped fresh lemon verbena

1 long strip lemon peel, crushed

1. In a large pot, bring the vinegar to a boil over medium heat and continue to boil for 3 minutes. Turn off the heat and add the lemon verbena and lemon peel. Cover the pot and allow the vinegar to cool for at least 1 hour.
2. Pour the cooled vinegar through a fine-mesh strainer into a very clean bottle and discard the solids. Store in a dark, dry place or in the refrigerator.

# SPICY BALSAMIC VINEGAR

*This vinegar is excellent on green salads and roasted bell pepper salad, as well as on others.*

### MAKES 3 CUPS

3 cups balsamic vinegar

3 garlic cloves, minced

1 long strip lemon peel, crushed

2 jalapeños, seeded and minced

1. In a large saucepan, bring the vinegar to boil over medium heat. Add the garlic, lemon peel, and peppers, reduce the heat to medium-low, and let cook for 5 minutes. Turn off the heat and allow it to cool for at least 1 hour.

2. Once the vinegar has cooled, pour it through a fine-mesh strainer into a very clean bottle and discard the solids. Store in a cool, dark place or in the refrigerator.

*A contented heart makes even the simplest food delicious.*

Zen proverb

# RASPBERRY-SCENTED VINEGAR

*This is a superb vinegar for green salads.*

MAKES 3 CUPS

**3 cups white wine vinegar**　　　　**1 tablespoon rum**
**1 cup fresh raspberries**

1. In a large pot, bring the vinegar to a boil over medium heat and continue to boil for about 3 minutes. Add the raspberries and rum, reduce the heat to low, and cook for about 2 more minutes. Turn off the heat. With the help of a masher, carefully crush the raspberries, then cover the pan and allow the vinegar to cool for at least 1 hour.

2. Pour the entire mixture into a clean, sterilized glass jar. A large canning jar is perfect for this. Refrigerate for 1 week.

3. After a week, pour the mixture through a fine-mesh strainer into a clean bottle, discarding the fruit. Store the bottle in a cool, dark place or refrigerate.

*Tranquility of soul consists in this alone,*
*To be united whole to God as one.*

Angelus Silesius

# SIMPLE VINAIGRETTE

## *(Vinaigrette Classique)*

MAKES ABOUT $^1/_2$ CUP

1 teaspoon salt

$^1/_2$ teaspoon freshly ground black pepper

2 tablespoons red wine vinegar

6 tablespoons extra virgin olive oil

Put the salt and pepper in a measuring cup or a bowl. Add the vinegar and stir thoroughly. Add the oil and stir some more, until all of the ingredients are completely blended.

VINAIGRETTE WITH MUSTARD *(VINAIGRETTE À LA MOUTARDE)*: Prepare the Simple Vinaigrette, then whisk in 1 tablespoon Dijon, Meaux, or another French mustard and mix thoroughly.

VINAIGRETTE WITH GARLIC *(VINAIGRETTE À L'AIL)*: Prepare the Simple Vinaigrette, then whisk in 1 crushed garlic clove. Let the vinaigrette stand for a few hours before using.

VINAIGRETTE WITH HERBS *(VINAIGRETTE AUX HERBES)*: Prepare the Simple Vinaigrette, substituting fresh lemon juice for the vinegar. Add $^1/_4$ cup finely chopped fresh herbs of your choice (such as parsley, tarragon, or cilantro) or scallions. Mix thoroughly.

# Spicy Spanish Vinaigrette

MAKES ABOUT 3/4 CUP

½ cup Spanish olive oil

3 tablespoons Spanish sherry vinegar (preferably Jerez)

½ teaspoon dried thyme

1 teaspoon sugar

1 teaspoon paprika

1 garlic clove, minced

1 scallion (white parts only), finely chopped

Salt and freshly ground black pepper to taste

Combine all the ingredients in a deep bowl and whisk together until the mixture thickens.

# Mayonnaise

Mayonnaise has many uses: Serve it with hard-boiled eggs, fold it into a potato salad, or spoon it over asparagus.

MAKES 1 CUP

1 very fresh egg yolk

1 teaspoon Dijon, Meaux, or another French mustard

1 teaspoon salt

½ teaspoon white pepper

About ¾ cup light olive oil or vegetable oil

2 teaspoons fresh lemon juice or tarragon vinegar

1. Put the egg yolk in a bowl. Add the mustard, salt, and pepper and begin to mix with a whisk or electric mixer (it is simpler with a mixer).
2. Add the oil little by little while continuing to mix. In between, add the lemon juice, then resume adding the oil and mixing until the mayonnaise thickens. Keep the mayonnaise in the refrigerator until ready to use. (Make it the day you plan to use it.)

# AIOLI MAYONNAISE

MAKES 1 CUP

2 very fresh egg yolks

4 garlic cloves, minced

1 tablespoon fresh lemon juice or tarragon vinegar

1 teaspoon Dijon mustard

Salt and white pepper to taste

1 cup light olive oil or vegetable oil

1. Put the egg yolks in a deep bowl. Add the garlic, lemon juice, and mustard, season with salt and pepper, and mix with a whisk or an electric mixer until uniform and creamy (it is simpler and quicker with a mixer).
2. Add the oil, a teaspoonful at a time, whisking or mixing until the aioli has thickened. Keep the aioli in the refrigerator until ready to use. (Make it the day you plan to use it.)

# BLUE CHEESE DRESSING

MAKES 1 1/2 CUPS

1/2 cup mayonnaise, homemade (page 238) or store-bought

1/3 cup heavy cream

1 teaspoon cider vinegar

1 tablespoon chopped fresh chives

1 1/2 ounces blue cheese (Bleu d'Auvergne, Stilton, Roquefort, or another blue cheese)

1. Combine the mayonnaise, cream, vinegar, and chives in a deep bowl. Blend with an electric mixer to achieve a uniform consistency.
2. Crumble the cheese into the mayonnaise mixture and stir thoroughly. Cover the bowl and refrigerate for at least 6 hours, or overnight, before using.

*Salad Oils, Vinegars,*
*and Dressings*

# THOUSAND ISLAND DRESSING

1 cup mayonnaise, homemade (page 238) or store-
bought

1/3 cup finely chopped pimento

3 tablespoons prepared chili sauce

2 tablespoons finely grated onion

2 tablespoons finely chopped green olives

1/4 cup milk (optional)

In a deep bowl, combine the mayonnaise, pimento, chili sauce, onion, and olives and mix well until uniform. If you prefer a thinner dressing, add the milk and continue to mix until well combined. Refrigerate for several hours before using.

# HONEY MUSTARD DRESSING

MAKES 3/4 CUP

1/2 cup light olive oil

3 tablespoons white wine vinegar

1 tablespoon Dijon, Meaux, or another French
mustard

1 tablespoon plus 2 teaspoons honey

2 tablespoons heavy cream (optional)

Salt and freshly ground black pepper to taste

Combine all the ingredients in a blender and whirl until smooth. Keep refrigerated until ready to use.

# CREAMY MUSTARD DRESSING

MAKES 1 CUP

$^1/_2$ cup heavy cream

1 very fresh egg yolk

$^1/_4$ cup light olive oil

1 tablespoon white wine vinegar

1 tablespoon Dijon, Meaux, or another French
mustard

1 teaspoon sugar

Salt and white pepper to taste

Combine all the ingredients in a blender and whirl until smooth. Refrigerate
for at least 3 hours before serving, and use the dressing the day you make it.

# FRENCH-STYLE HERB DRESSING

MAKES 1 CUP

$^3/_4$ cup heavy cream

2 tablespoons olive oil

2 tablespoons finely chopped fresh basil

2 tablespoons finely chopped fresh chervil or
Italian parsley

2 tablespoons finely chopped fresh chives

1 shallot, minced

1 garlic clove, minced

Salt and white pepper to taste

Combine all the ingredients in a blender and whirl until a smooth and uniform consistency is achieved. Refrigerate until ready to use.

# FRENCH-STYLE CREAMY LEMON DRESSING

MAKES 3/4 CUP

½ cup heavy cream

5 tablespoons olive oil

Juice from 1 lemon

Salt and white pepper to taste

Combine all the ingredients in a blender and whirl until smooth. Refrigerate for several hours before using.

# FRENCH-STYLE ROQUEFORT DRESSING

MAKES 2/3 CUP

¼ cup plain low-fat yogurt

¼ cup heavy cream

2 tablespoons olive oil

2 tablespoons white wine vinegar

Salt and white pepper to taste

2 ounces Roquefort cheese, crumbled

Combine all the ingredients, except the cheese, in a deep bowl. Beat with an electric mixer until the dressing is smooth and creamy. Add the crumbled cheese and mix well with a fork or spoon. Refrigerate for several hours before using.

*Simplicity reaches out to God,*
*Purity of heart discovers and enjoys Him.*

Thomas à Kempis

# Tarragon Sauce "Classique"

## (Sauce à l'Estragon)

MAKES 1 CUP

½ cup sour cream

3 tablespoons fresh lemon juice

½ cup heavy cream

3 tablespoons chopped fresh tarragon

Salt and freshly ground black pepper
   to taste

Combine all the ingredients in a deep bowl and beat with an electric mixer until well mixed. Refrigerate until ready to use.

# Festive Dressing

*Try this on salads containing melon and other fresh fruits.*

MAKES ²/₃ CUP

½ cup light olive oil

¼ cup dry white wine or dry sherry

1 tablespoon fresh lemon juice

1 teaspoon dry mustard

1 teaspoon celery seeds

1 tablespoon sugar

Pinch of salt

Combine all the ingredients in a blender and whirl until uniform and smooth. Refrigerate until ready to use.

# HONEY LEMON DRESSING

*This is another great dressing for fruit salads.*

MAKES 1 CUP

½ cup light olive oil

¼ cup fresh lemon juice

3 tablespoons honey, or more to taste

One 3-ounce package cream cheese,
cut into small pieces

Dash of cayenne pepper

Pinch of salt

Combine all the ingredients in a blender and whirl until uniform and smooth. Taste and adjust the seasonings. Refrigerate until ready to use.

# SPICY NAPOLEON SAUCE

*This is excellent served over cold vegetables or cold poached salmon.*

MAKES A SCANT 1½ CUPS

2 tablespoons fresh lemon juice

1¼ cups plain yogurt or low-fat
sour cream

½ teaspoon Dijon, Meaux, or
another French mustard

½ teaspoon curry powder

½ teaspoon paprika

½ teaspoon ground cumin

½ teaspoon ground coriander

1 garlic clove, finely minced

Pinch of salt

Cayenne pepper to taste

Combine all the ingredients in a deep bowl and blend well with an electric mixer, whisk, or fork until smooth and well blended. Refrigerate until ready to use.

# MEASUREMENT EQUIVALENTS

*Please note that all conversions are approximate.*

## Liquid Conversions

| U.S. | METRIC | U.S. | METRIC |
|---|---|---|---|
| 1 tsp | 5 ml | 1 cup + 2 tbs | 275 ml |
| 1 tbs | 15 ml | 1¼ cups | 300 ml |
| 2 tbs | 30 ml | 1⅓ cups | 325 ml |
| 3 tbs | 45 ml | 1½ cups | 350 ml |
| ¼ cup | 60 ml | 1⅔ cups | 375 ml |
| ⅓ cup | 75 ml | 1¾ cups | 400 ml |
| ⅓ cup + 1 tbs | 90 ml | 1¾ cups + 2 tbs | 450 ml |
| ⅓ cup + 2 tbs | 100 ml | 2 cups (1 pint) | 475 ml |
| ½ cup | 120 ml | 2½ cups | 600 ml |
| ⅔ cup | 150 ml | 3 cups | 720 ml |
| ¾ cup | 180 ml | 4 cups (1 quart) | 945 ml |
| ¾ cup + 2 tbs | 200 ml | | (1,000 ml |
| 1 cup | 240 ml | | is 1 liter) |

## Weight Conversions

| US/UK | METRIC | US/UK | METRIC |
|---|---|---|---|
| ½ oz | 14 g | 7 oz | 200 g |
| 1 oz | 28 g | 8 oz | 227 g |
| 1½ oz | 48 g | 9 oz | 255 g |
| 2 oz | 57 g | 10 oz | 284 g |
| 2½ oz | 66 g | 11 oz | 312 g |
| 3 oz | 85 g | 12 oz | 340 g |
| 3½ oz | 100 g | 13 oz | 368 g |
| 4 oz | 113 g | 14 oz | 400 g |
| 5 oz | 142 g | 15 oz | 425 g |
| 6 oz | 170 g | 1 lb | 454 g |

## Oven Temperatures

| F | GAS MARK | C | F | GAS MARK | C |
|---|---|---|---|---|---|
| 250 | ½ | 120 | 400 | 6 | 200 |
| 275 | 1 | 140 | 425 | 7 | 220 |
| 300 | 2 | 150 | 450 | 8 | 230 |
| 325 | 3 | 165 | 475 | 9 | 240 |
| 350 | 4 | 180 | 500 | 10 | 260 |
| 375 | 5 | 190 | 550 | Broil | 290 |

# INDEX

## A

Aioli Mayonnaise, 239
All-American Tossed Salad, 101
Almonds
    Immaculata Salad, 224
    Madagascar Date-Nut Salad, 48
    Stuffed Avocado Salad, 225
    Wild Rice and Barley Salad, 35
Ancient Persian Salad, 13
Apple(s)
    Bar-Le-Duc Salad, 22
    Cabbage, and Pineapple Slaw, 161
    Clementine, and Spinach Salad,
        226
    Endive Salad with Blue Cheese, 34
    Immaculata Salad, 224
    Madagascar Date-Nut Salad, 48
    Mayfair Salad, 30
    Mixed Jicama Salad, 140
    Orange, and Endive Salad, 23
    Orange, and Fennel Salad, 227
    Oriental Salad, 9
    Quick Belgian-Style Salad, 198
    Rainbow Salad, 193
    Red Beet Salad with Roquefort
        Cheese, 182
    Russian Fruit and Vegetable Salad,
        183
    *Salade Savoyarde*, 167
    and Smoked Salmon Appetizer, 204
    Tangy Fruit Salad, 172
    Taramasalata Egg Salad, 72
    Tutti-Frutti Salad, 194
    Venetian Gorgonzola Salad, 32
    Waldorf Salad, 31
Artichoke(s)
    Etruscan Salad, 45
    Heart Salad, 221
    Salad, Greek-Style, 69
    *Salade Rachel*, 94
Arugula, 3
    and Dandelion Salad with Roasted
        Pears, 89

Dutchess County Crispy Salad with
    Blue Cheese Dressing, 178
Fresh Greens and Tuna Salad, 108
Garden Greens and Herb Salad,
    100
Garden Salad with *Sauce au
    Caviar*, 44
Immaculata Salad, 224
Italian Winter Salad, 38
Mixed Green Salad Provençal, 144
and Mushroom Salad, 80
Orecchiette, and Radicchio Salad,
    188
Persimmon and Greens Salad, 195
Roman Mixed Salad, 62
St. Mary Magdalene Salad, 128
Venetian Gorgonzola Salad, 32
Asparagus
    Beet, and Egg Salad, 84
    Madrid Mixed Salad, 154
    *Salade Rachel*, 94
Assumpta Salad, 146
Avocado(s)
    Boston Salad, 16
    Copperfield Salad, 33
    Dutchess County Crispy Salad with
        Blue Cheese Dressing, 178
    and Egg Appetizer Salad, 26
    Gazpacho Salad, 138
    and Goat Cheese Salad, 78
    Guacamole Salad, 163
    and Jicama Salad, 36
    and Mushroom Salad, 98
    and Orange Salad, 228
    Pinoche Pasta Salad, 46
    Rainbow Salad, 193
    *Salade Camille*, 124
    and Salmon Salad, 52
    St. Andrew "The First Called"
        Salad, 209
    St. Fiacre Salad, 148
    St. Martin Salad, 211
    Stuffed, Salad, 225

Taramasalata Egg Salad, 72
and Watercress Salad, 184

## B

Baby chicory, 2
    Egg, Celery, and Radish Salad with
        Tarragon Sauce, 49
    French Mimosa Salad, 56
    Fresh Greens and Tuna Salad, 108
    Frisée and Bleu d'Auvergne Salad,
        19
    Garden Greens and Herb Salad,
        100
    Italian Salad with Cooked
        Dandelion Greens, 107
    Italian Summer Salad, 122
    Mixed Green Salad Provençal, 144
    Orange, Apple, and Endive Salad,
        23
    Peach and Chicory Salad, 150
    Pear and Watercress Salad, 212
    Persimmon and Greens Salad, 195
    Roasted Red Pepper, Chicory, and
        Mozzarella Salad, 83
    Roman Mixed Salad, 62
    *Salade au Roquefort*, 77
    *Salade Composée*, 156
    Venetian Gorgonzola Salad, 32
Bacon
    Fresh Dandelion Salad, 63
    Italian Salad with Cooked
        Dandelion Greens, 107
Balsamic Vinegar, Spicy, 235
Bananas
    Tutti-Frutti Salad, 194
Bar-Le-Duc Salad, 22
Barley and Wild Rice Salad, 35
Basil
    -Scented Vinegar, 234
    Assumpta Salad, 146
    Farfalle and Chickpea Salad, 91
    Italian Summer Salad, 122
    Italian Tomato Salad, 142

Basil *(cont.)*
    Mount St.-Michel Egg Salad, 104
    Pesto-Filled Deviled Eggs, 105
    *Salade Niçoise*, 135
    St. Michael's Salad, 170
    Tomato, Onion, and Mozzarella
        Salad, 143
    Tomato and Olive Salad from the
        Lazio, 120
    Tuscan Salad, 123
Bean sprouts
    Japanese Sprout Salad, 11
    Oriental Salad, 9
    Sts. Peter and Paul Salad, 111
Bean(s)
    Black, Salad, Mexican Style, Spicy,
        134
    Black-Eyed Pea Salad, Portuguese
        Style, 158
    Chickpea Salad, 164
    Chickpea Salad, Spanish Style, 176
    Etruscan Salad, 45
    Farfalle and Chickpea Salad, 91
    Fava, Salad, Campania, 65
    Fava, Salad Egyptian Style, 64
    Green, and Macaroni Salad, 203
    Green, and Tomato Salad, 179
    Indian Curried Lentil Salad, 219
    Lentil Salad, Cantal Style, 90
    Mediterranean Lentil and Rice
        Salad, 201
    Mixed, Salad, Spicy, 18
    Pole, Salad, 166
    and Potato Salad, Sicilian, 121
    Prophet Elijah Lentil Salad, 127
    Salad, Northern Italian, 75
    Salad, South American, 218
    *Salade Bonne Femme*, 109
    *Salade Composée*, 156
    *Salade Landaise*, 189
    St. Anne Salad, 130
    St. Fiacre Salad, 148
    St. Joaquim Salad, 129
    St. John the Baptist Potato Salad,
        110
    Transfiguration Salad, 137
Beet(s)
    Asparagus, and Egg Salad, 84
    Baby, Potato, and Onion Salad, 162
    Chilled Amber Salad, 180

Dutch-Style Egg and Cheese Salad,
    51
New York Columbia County Salad,
    200
Red, Salad with Roquefort Cheese,
    182
Rémoulade, Monastery, 202
and Rémoulade Sauce, Capered
    Deviled Eggs with, 20
Russian Potato Salad, 114
St. Francis Salad, 192
St. Joaquim Salad, 129
Belgian endives, 3
    Arugula and Dandelion Salad with
        Roasted Pears, 89
    Avocado and Egg Appetizer Salad,
        26
    Bar-Le-Duc Salad, 22
    Belgian Salad, 12
    Dutch-Style Egg and Cheese Salad,
        51
    Dutchess County Crispy Salad with
        Blue Cheese Dressing, 178
    Endive Salad with Blue Cheese, 34
    Farnese Salad, 55
    French Mimosa Salad, 56
    Herbed Tofu Salad, 215
    Mango Salad Piquant, 112
    Mixed Green Salad Provençal, 144
    Orange, Apple, and Endive Salad,
        23
    Orange and Avocado Salad, 228
    Papaya and Endive Salad in
        Rémoulade Sauce, 47
    Pear, Endive, and Brie Salad, 17
    Persimmon and Greens Salad, 195
    Pickled Deviled Egg Salad, 40
    Quick Belgian-Style Salad, 198
    Red Beet Salad with Roquefort
        Cheese, 182
    *Salade Nivernaise*, 206
    St. Francis Salad, 192
    St. Hildegarde's Salad, 169
    St. Martin Salad, 211
    Venetian Gorgonzola Salad, 32
Belgian Salad, 12
Berried Smoked Salmon Salad, 171
Bibb lettuce, 2
    French Mimosa Salad, 56
Bistro Egg Salad, 50

Black-Eyed Pea Salad, Portuguese
    Style, 158
Blue Cheese
    Caesar Salad, 8
    Dressing, 239
    Dressing, Creamy, 41
    Endive Salad with, 34
    French-Style Roquefort Dressing,
        242
    Frisée and Bleu d'Auvergne Salad,
        19
    Immaculata Salad, 224
    Pear and Watercress Salad, 212
    Persimmon and Greens Salad, 195
    Quick Belgian-Style Salad, 198
    Rainbow Salad, 193
    Red Beet Salad with Roquefort
        Cheese, 182
    Roquefort Mayonnaise, 23
    Salad from the Auvergne, 205
    *Salade au Roquefort*, 77
    *Salade Picarde*, 57
    St. Scholastica Salad, 41
    Venetian Gorgonzola Salad, 32
Blueberries
    Berried Smoked Salmon Salad, 171
    Heavenly Fruit Salad with
        Camembert, 174
    Kiwi and Peach Salad, 151
    Riviera Cantaloupe Salad, 149
    Summer Fruit Platter, 132
    Summertime Salad, 152
Bon Appétit Salad, 67
Boston lettuce, 2
    Avocado and Goat Cheese Salad,
        78
    Boston Salad, 16
    Caesar Salad, 8
    Fresh Dandelion Salad, 63
    Garden Greens and Herb Salad, 100
    Herbed Tofu Salad, 215
    Immaculata Salad, 224
    Italian Mixed Salad, 87
    Madrid Mixed Salad, 154
    Oriental Salad, 9
    *Salade au Roquefort*, 77
    *Salade Niçoise*, 135
    Salmon and Avocado Salad, 52
    Salmon and Cucumber Salad, 73
Boston Salad, 16

Bread (in salads)
  Bistro Egg Salad, 50
  Caesar Salad, 8
  Frisée and Bleu D'Auvergne Salad, 19
  Paradiso Salad, 53
  Provençal Mesclun Salad, 92
  Salad from the Auvergne, 205
  *Salade Landaise*, 189
  Tuscan Salad, 123
Brie, Pear, and Endive Salad, 17
Broccoli
  Cauliflower, and Jicama in Yogurt Dressing, 160
  and Rigatoni Salad, 187
  *Salade Campagnarde*, 208
Bulgur
  and Cherry Tomatoes Salad, 185
  Middle Eastern Tabbouleh Salad, 115
Butterhead lettuce, 2. *See also* Boston lettuce
  French Mimosa Salad, 56
  Fresh Dandelion Salad, 63
  Italian Mixed Salad, 87
  Madrid Mixed Salad, 154

C
Cabbage
  Apple, and Pineapple Slaw, 161
  Bon Appétit Salad, 67
  Chilled Amber Salad, 180
  Emerald Salad, Indonesian Style, 99
  green, about, 4
  Monastery-Style Coleslaw, 222
  red, about, 4
  Room-Temperature Red Salad, 216
  *Salade des Crudités*, 145
  *Salade Picarde*, 57
  *Salade Savoyarde*, 167
  Two, Salad, 14
Caesar Salad, 8
Camembert, Heavenly Fruit Salad with, 174
Campania Fava Bean Salad, 65
Cantaloupe
  Salad, Riviera, 149
  Summertime Salad, 152
Capers
  Capered Deviled Eggs with Beets and Rémoulade Sauce, 20

Eggs Tonnato, 70
Israeli Salad, 139
Mushroom and Avocado Salad, 98
Potato Salad Holy Elder Simeon, 191
Roasted Sweet Pepper Salad from the Piedmont, 220
Salmon and Avocado Salad, 52
Savory Cauliflower Salad, 27
Sicilian Bean and Potato Salad, 121
Sicilian Potato Salad, 54
St. Basil Macaroni Salad, 168
Carrot(s)
  Ancient Persian Salad, 13
  Bar-Le-Duc Salad, 22
  and Black Olive Salad, 190
  Bon Appétit Salad, 67
  Emerald Salad, Indonesian Style, 99
  Italian Mixed Salad, 87
  Mexican Salad, 199
  Monastery-Style Coleslaw, 222
  Northern Italian Bean Salad, 75
  Potato Salad, Tuscan Style, 74
  Rainbow Salad, 193
  Russian Fruit and Vegetable Salad, 183
  Russian Potato Salad, 114
  Salad, Chilled, 82
  Salad, Spartan, 66
  *Salade Composée*, 156
  *Salade des Crudités*, 145
  *Salade Savoyarde*, 167
  St. Martin Salad, 211
  Two Cabbages Salad, 14
Catfish Salad, Greek Style, 106
Cauliflower
  Broccoli, and Jicama in Yogurt Dressing, 160
  Salad, Savory, 27
  Salad, St. Cecile, 210
  *Salade Campagnarde*, 208
  *Salade du Barry*, 93
  *Salade Nivernaise*, 206
  *Salade Picarde*, 57
  St. Joaquim Salad, 129
*Caviar, Sauce au*, 44
Celery
  Egg, and Radish Salad with Tarragon Sauce, 49
  Macaroni Salad, 119

Madagascar Date-Nut Salad, 48
Northern Italian Bean Salad, 75
Savory Potato Salad, 37
Celery root
  Potato Salad, Tuscan Style, 74
  Waldorf Salad, 31
Cheddar, Egg, and Rice Salad, 85
Cheese. *See also* Blue Cheese; Goat Cheese; Mozzarella
  Assumpta Salad, 146
  Caesar Salad, 8
  Catfish Salad, Greek Style, 106
  Egg, Cheddar, and Rice Salad, 85
  and Egg Salad, Dutch-Style, 51
  Etruscan Salad, 45
  Heavenly Fruit Salad with Camembert, 174
  Horiatiki Greek Salad, 155
  Mediterranean Lentil and Rice Salad, 201
  Paradiso Salad, 53
  Pear, Endive, and Brie Salad, 17
  Roasted Sweet Pepper Salad from the Piedmont, 220
  Salad from the Auvergne, 205
  *Salade Campagnarde*, 208
  *Salade Landaise*, 189
  Salmon and Cucumber Salad, 73
  St. Hildegarde's Salad, 169
  Stuffed Melon Salad, 131
  Valle D'Aosta Salad, 103
Cherry Tomatoes and Bulgur Salad, 185
Chickpea(s)
  and Farfalle Salad, 91
  Northern Italian Bean Salad, 75
  Salad, 164
  Salad, Spanish Style, 176
  St. John the Baptist Potato Salad, 110
  Transfiguration Salad, 137
Chicory, 2
  Cooked Fennel Salad, 181
Chicory, baby. *See* Baby chicory
Chilled Amber Salad, 180
Chilled Carrot Salad, 82
Cilantro
  Avocado and Goat Cheese Salad, 78
  Garden Greens and Herb Salad, 100
  Gazpacho Salad, 138

Cilantro (cont.)
  Green Bean and Tomato Salad, 179
  Jicama and Avocado Salad, 36
  Orange and Avocado Salad, 228
  Prophet Elijah Lentil Salad, 127
  Spicy Black Bean Salad, Mexican
    Style, 134
  St. Fiacre Salad, 148
Citrus-Scented Oil, 233
Clementine, Apple, and Spinach
  Salad, 226
Coconut
  Emerald Salad, Indonesian Style, 99
  Fruit Relish Salad, 173
Cold Egg, Potato, and Tuna Salad with
  Mustard-Tarragon Dressing, 71
Cooked Fennel Salad, 181
Copperfield Salad, 33
Corn
  Mexican Salad, 199
  Spicy Black Bean Salad, Mexican
    Style, 134
  Spicy Mixed Bean Salad, 18
Costa Brava Egg-and-Tuna Filled
  Tomatoes, 117
Couscous Salad, Crunchy, 177
Creamy Mustard Dressing, 241
Croutons
  Bistro Egg Salad, 50
  Caesar Salad, 8
  Frisée and Bleu D'Auvergne Salad,
    19
  Paradiso Salad, 53
  Salad from the Auvergne, 205
  Salade Landaise, 189
Crunchy Couscous Salad, 177
Cucumber(s)
  All-American Tossed Salad, 101
  Ancient Persian Salad, 13
  Baby Spinach and Orange Salad, 15
  Broccoli, Cauliflower, and Jicama in
    Yogurt Dressing, 160
  Cherry Tomatoes and Bulgur Salad,
    185
  Chickpea Salad, 164
  Chickpea Salad, Spanish Style, 176
  Cooked Fennel Salad, 181
  Costa Brava Egg-and-Tuna Filled
    Tomatoes, 117
  Crunchy Couscous Salad, 177

Gazpacho Salad, 138
German Potato Salad, 10
Indian Curried Lentil Salad, 219
Israeli Salad, 139
Italian Mixed Salad, 87
Italian Summer Salad, 122
Lentil Salad, Cantal Style, 90
Madagascar Date-Nut Salad, 48
Mayfair Salad, 30
Mediterranean Lentil and Rice
  Salad, 201
Middle Eastern Tabbouleh Salad,
  115
Mint-Flavored Fusilli Salad, 118
Mixed Jicama Salad, 140
Mount St.-Michel Egg Salad, 104
Penne Salad, 186
Salade des Crudités, 145
Salade Niçoise, 135
Salade Picarde, 57
and Salmon Salad, 73
Savory Potato Salad, 37
Spanish Salad, 136
St. Benedict Salad, 126
Tangy Fruit Salad, 172
Taramasalata Egg Salad, 72
Tuscan Salad, 123
Tuscan Stuffed Tomato Salad, 159
Curried Lentil Salad, Indian, 219
Curry Mayonnaise, 126

D
Dandelion Greens, 3
  and Arugula Salad with Roasted
    Pears, 89
  Cooked, Italian Salad with, 107
  Fresh, Salad, 63
  Persimmon and Greens Salad, 195
  Roman Mixed Salad, 62
Date(s)
  -Nut Salad, Madagascar, 48
  Orange, Apple, and Fennel Salad,
    227
Dressings. See also Vinaigrette;
    individual salad recipes
  Aioli Mayonnaise, 239
  Blue Cheese, 239
  Creamy Blue Cheese, 41
  Creamy Mustard, 241
  Curry Mayonnaise, 126

Festive, 243
French Deluxe, 127, 209
French-Style Creamy Lemon, 242
French-Style Herb, 241
French-Style Roquefort, 242
Honey Lemon, 244
Honey Mustard, 240
Light Mayonnaise, 190
Mayonnaise, 238
Mustard-Tarragon, 71
preparing, 229–230
Rémoulade, 31
Rémoulade Sauce, 20, 47, 202
Roquefort Mayonnaise, 23
Sauce au Caviar, 44
Spicy Napoleon Sauce, 244
Tarragon Sauce, 49
Tarragon Sauce "Classique," 243
Thousand Island, 240
Tonnato Sauce, 70
Yogurt, 160
Dutch-Style Egg and Cheese Salad, 51
Dutchess County Crispy Salad with
  Blue Cheese Dressing, 178

E
Egg(s)
  -and-Tuna Filled Tomatoes, Costa
    Brava, 117
  Artichoke Heart Salad, 221
  Asparagus, and Beet Salad, 84
  and Avocado Appetizer Salad, 26
  Belgian Salad, 12
  Black-Eyed Pea Salad, Portuguese
    Style, 158
  Caesar Salad, 8
  Campania Fava Bean Salad, 65
  Capered Deviled, with Beets and
    Rémoulade Sauce, 20
  Celery, and Radish Salad with
    Tarragon Sauce, 49
  Cheddar, and Rice Salad, 85
  and Cheese Salad, Dutch-Style, 51
  Clementine, Apple, and Spinach
    Salad, 226
  Deviled, Pesto-Filled, 105
  Deviled, Salad, Monastery, 21
  Deviled Pickled, Salad, 40
  Fava Bean Salad Egyptian Style, 64
  French Mimosa Salad, 56

Late-Summer Tomato and Parsley
 Salad, 165
Macaroni Salad, 119
Madrid Mixed Salad, 154
Plain Leek Salad, 39
Potato, and Tuna Salad, Cold, with
 Mustard-Tarragon Dressing, 71
Potato Salad Holy Elder Simeon, 191
Potato Salad Mont-Blanc, 157
Russian Potato Salad, 114
Salad, Bistro, 50
Salad, Mount St.-Michel, 104
Salad, Taramasalata, 72
Salad from the Auvergne, 205
*Salade Bonne Femme*, 109
*Salade Camille*, 124
*Salade Nantaise*, 223
*Salade Niçoise*, 135
*Salade Nivernaise*, 206
*Salade Picarde*, 57
*Salade Rachel*, 94
Savory Cauliflower Salad, 27
South American Bean Salad, 218
and Spinach Salad, 86
St. Andrew "The First Called"
 Salad, 209
St. Basil Macaroni Salad, 168
St. Joseph Salad, 58
Sts. Peter and Paul Salad, 111
Tomato Salad, Alsatian Style, 116
Tonnato, 70
Emerald Salad, Indonesian Style, 99
Endive. *See* Belgian endives
Escarole, 2
 Asparagus, Beet, and Egg Salad, 84
 Horiatiki Greek Salad, 155
 Salad from the Auvergne, 205
Etruscan Salad, 45

F
Farfalle and Chickpea Salad, 91
Farnese Salad, 55
Fava Bean(s)
 Etruscan Salad, 45
 Salad, Campania, 65
 Salad Egyptian Style, 64
Fennel
 Cabbage, Apple, and Pineapple
  Slaw, 161
 Cooked, Salad, 181

Farnese Salad, 55
Italian Winter Salad, 38
Mayfair Salad, 30
Mint-Flavored Fusilli Salad, 118
Mushroom Salad, Greek Style, 214
Orange, and Apple Salad, 227
Prophet Elijah Lentil Salad, 127
Roman Mixed Salad, 62
Salad, Perugia, 28
St. Fiacre Salad, 148
St. Scholastica Salad, 41
Sts. Peter and Paul Salad, 111
Valle D'Aosta Salad, 103
Festive Dressing, 243
Feta cheese
 Assumpta Salad, 146
 Catfish Salad, Greek Style, 106
 Horiatiki Greek Salad, 155
 Mediterranean Lentil and Rice
  Salad, 201
 Salmon and Cucumber Salad, 73
Fish
 Berried Smoked Salmon Salad, 171
 Catfish Salad, Greek Style, 106
 Cold Egg, Potato, and Tuna Salad
  with Mustard-Tarragon Dressing,
  71
 Costa Brava Egg-and-Tuna Filled
  Tomatoes, 117
 Eggs Tonnato, 70
 Fresh Greens and Tuna Salad, 108
 Madrid Mixed Salad, 154
 Paradiso Salad, 53
 *Salade Camille*, 124
 *Salade Niçoise*, 135
 Salmon and Avocado Salad, 52
 Salmon and Cucumber Salad, 73
 *Sauce au Caviar*, 44
 Smoked Salmon and Apple
  Appetizer, 204
 St. Andrew "The First Called"
  Salad, 209
French Deluxe Dressing, 127, 209
French Mimosa Salad, 56
French-Style Creamy Lemon
 Dressing, 242
French-Style Herb Dressing, 241
French-Style Roquefort Dressing, 242
Frisée. *See* Baby chicory
Fruit. *See also specific fruits*

Platter, Summer, 132
Relish Salad, 173
Salad, Heavenly, with Camembert,
 174
Salad, Royal, 42
Salad, Tangy, 172
and Vegetable Salad, Russian, 183
Fusilli (pasta)
 Etruscan Salad, 45
 Salad, Mint-Flavored, 118

G
Garden Greens and Herb Salad, 100
Garden Salad with *Sauce au Caviar*,
 44
Garlic, Vinaigrette with, 237
Gazpacho Salad, 138
German Potato Salad, 10
Goat Cheese
 and Avocado Salad, 78
 New York Columbia County Salad,
  200
 Peach and Chicory Salad, 150
 Provençal Mesclun Salad, 92
 St. Mary Magdalene Salad, 128
 Stuffed Avocado Salad, 225
Gorgonzola
 Pear and Watercress Salad, 212
 Rainbow Salad, 193
 Salad, Venetian, 32
Grapefruit
 Bar-Le-Duc Salad, 22
Grapes
 Fruit Relish Salad, 173
 Orange, Apple, and Endive Salad, 23
 Rainbow Salad, 193
 Regina Salad, 147
 Riviera Cantaloupe Salad, 149
Greek-Style Artichoke Salad, 69
Greek Vinaigrette, 106
greens, salad, 1–4. *See also* Lettuce;
  *specific types*
 tearing into pieces, 4
 washing, 4
Guacamole Salad, 163

H
Ham
 Salad from the Auvergne, 205
 *Salade Nivernaise*, 206

Hazelnuts
  *Salade Poitevine*, 207
Heavenly Fruit Salad with
    Camembert, 174
Herb(s). *See also specific herbs*
  -Scented Oil, 232
  Dressing, French-Style, 241
  and Garden Greens Salad, 100
  Herbed Tofu Salad, 215
  Savory Potato Salad, 37
  Vinaigrette with, 237
Honey Lemon Dressing, 244
Honey Mustard Dressing, 240
Horiatiki Greek Salad, 155

I

iceberg lettuce, about, 2
Immaculata Salad, 224
Indian Curried Lentil Salad, 219
Israeli Salad, 139
Italian Mixed Salad, 87
Italian Salad with Cooked Dandelion
    Greens, 107
Italian Summer Salad, 122
Italian Tomato Salad, 142
Italian Winter Salad, 38

J

Japanese Sprout Salad, 11
Jicama
  and Avocado Salad, 36
  Broccoli, and Cauliflower in Yogurt
    Dressing, 160
  Salad, Mixed, 140

K

Kiwi and Peach Salad, 151

L

Late-Summer Tomato and Parsley
    Salad, 165
Leek Salad, Plain, 39
Lemon Verbena–Scented Vinegar,
    234
Lentil(s)
  and Rice Salad, Mediterranean, 201
  Salad, Cantal Style, 90
  Salad, Indian Curried, 219
  Salad, Prophet Elijah, 127
  St. Anne Salad, 130

Lettuce. *See also specific types*
  Dutchess County Crispy Salad with
    Blue Cheese Dressing, 178
  New York Columbia County Salad,
    200
  types of, 2
Lolla Rossa greens, 1

M

Macaroni
  and Green Bean Salad, 203
  Salad, 119
  Salad, St. Basil, 168
Mâche, 3
  French Mimosa Salad, 56
  *Salade Croquante*, 76
  *Salade Nantaise*, 223
  Smoked Salmon and Apple
    Appetizer, 204
  St. Mary Magdalene Salad, 128
Madagascar Date-Nut Salad, 48
Madrid Mixed Salad, 154
Mango Salad Piquant, 112
Marinated Roasted Pepper Salad, 29
Mayfair Salad, 30
Mayonnaise, 238
  Aioli, 239
  Curry, 126
  Dressing, Light, 190
  Rémoulade Dressing, 31
  Rémoulade Sauce, 20, 47, 202
  Roquefort, 23
Mediterranean Lentil and Rice Salad,
    201
Melon
  Fruit Relish Salad, 173
  Rainbow Salad, 193
  Riviera Cantaloupe Salad, 149
  Royal Fruit Salad, 42
  Stuffed, Salad, 131
  Summer Fruit Platter, 132
  Summertime Salad, 152
Mesclun, 2
  Bon Appétit Salad, 67
  Salad, Provençal, 92
  *Salade Croquante*, 76
Mexican Salad, 199
Middle Eastern Tabbouleh Salad, 115
Mint
  -Flavored Fusilli Salad, 118

Cherry Tomatoes and Bulgur Salad,
    185
  Emerald Salad, Indonesian Style, 99
  Middle Eastern Tabbouleh Salad, 115
  Orange and Tangerine Salad, 95
  Royal Fruit Salad, 42
Mixed Green Salad Provençal, 144
Mixed Jicama Salad, 140
Monastery Beet Rémoulade, 202
Monastery Deviled Egg Salad, 21
Monastery-Style Coleslaw, 222
Mount St.-Michel Egg Salad, 104
Mozzarella
  Rigatoni and Broccoli Salad, 187
  Roasted Red Pepper, and Chicory
    Salad, 83
  St. Michael's Salad, 170
  Tomato, and Onion Salad, 143
  Tomato and Olive Salad from the
    Lazio, 120
Mushroom(s)
  and Arugula Salad, 80
  and Avocado Salad, 98
  Salad, Greek Style, 214
  *Salade Bonne Femme*, 109
  *Salade Campagnarde*, 208
  *Salade Poitevine*, 207
  St. Andrew "The First Called"
    Salad, 209
  St. Martin Salad, 211
Mustard, Vinaigrette with, 237
Mustard Dressing, Creamy, 241
Mustard Dressing, Honey, 240
Mustard-Tarragon Dressing, 71

N

New York Columbia County Salad,
    200
Northern Italian Bean Salad, 75
Nuts. *See also* Almonds; Pecans;
    Walnuts
  *Salade Poitevine*, 207

O

Oil, Citrus-Scented, 233
Oil, Herb-Scented, 232
Oil, Spicy, 233
Olive(s)
  Assumpta Salad, 146
  Black, and Carrot Salad, 190

Campania Fava Bean Salad, 65
Catfish Salad, Greek Style, 106
Chickpea Salad, Spanish Style, 176
Chilled Amber Salad, 180
Copperfield Salad, 33
Costa Brava Egg-and-Tuna Filled
    Tomatoes, 117
Egg, Cheddar, and Rice Salad, 85
Gazpacho Salad, 138
Horiatiki Greek Salad, 155
Israeli Salad, 139
Late-Summer Tomato and Parsley
    Salad, 165
Macaroni and Green Bean Salad, 203
Macaroni Salad, 119
Madrid Mixed Salad, 154
Marinated Roasted Pepper Salad, 29
Mediterranean Lentil and Rice
    Salad, 201
Mount St.-Michel Egg Salad, 104
Orange, Apple, and Endive Salad, 23
Orange and Tangerine Salad, 95
Orecchiette, Arugula, and
    Radicchio Salad, 188
Orzo and Green Pea Salad, 102
Penne Salad, 186
Perugia Fennel Salad, 28
Pesto-Filled Deviled Eggs, 105
Pinoche Pasta Salad, 46
Potato Salad Holy Elder Simeon,
    191
Rigatoni and Broccoli Salad, 187
Roasted Sweet Pepper Salad from
    the Piedmont, 220
Russian Potato Salad, 114
Salade Camille, 124
Salade Composée, 156
Salade du Barry, 93
Salade Niçoise, 135
Sevilla Salad, 68
Sicilian Bean and Potato Salad, 121
Sicilian Potato Salad, 54
Spanish Salad, 136
St. Benedict Salad, 126
St. John the Baptist Potato Salad,
    110
St. Michael's Salad, 170
Stuffed Avocado Salad, 225
and Tomato Salad from the Lazio,
    120

Tuscan Salad, 123
Valle D'Aosta Salad, 103
Onion, Roasted, Salad, 217
Orange(s)
    Apple, and Endive Salad, 23
    Apple, and Fennel Salad, 227
    and Avocado Salad, 228
    and Baby Spinach Salad, 15
    Belgian Salad, 12
    Berried Smoked Salmon Salad, 171
    Boston Salad, 16
    Chilled Amber Salad, 180
    Clementine, Apple, and Spinach
        Salad, 226
    Copperfield Salad, 33
    Farnese Salad, 55
    Room-Temperature Red Salad, 216
    Royal Fruit Salad, 42
    Sevilla Salad, 68
    Summer Fruit Platter, 132
    and Tangerine Salad, 95
    Tangy Fruit Salad, 172
Orecchiette, Arugula, and Radicchio
    Salad, 188
Oriental Salad, 9
Orzo and Green Pea Salad, 102

P

Papaya
    and Endive Salad in Rémoulade
        Sauce, 47
    Tutti-Frutti Salad, 194
Paradiso Salad, 53
Parmesan cheese
    Caesar Salad, 8
    Paradiso Salad, 53
Parsley and Tomato Salad, Late-
    Summer, 165
Pasta
    Etruscan Salad, 45
    Farfalle and Chickpea Salad, 91
    Macaroni and Green Bean Salad,
        203
    Macaroni Salad, 119
    Mint-Flavored Fusilli Salad, 118
    Orecchiette, Arugula, and
        Radicchio Salad, 188
    Orzo and Green Pea Salad, 102
    Penne Salad, 186
    Rigatoni and Broccoli Salad, 187

Rotelle in Spicy Napoleon Sauce,
    141
Salad, Pinoche, 46
St. Basil Macaroni Salad, 168
Peach(es)
    and Chicory Salad, 150
    Fruit Relish Salad, 173
    and Kiwi Salad, 151
    Summer Fruit Platter, 132
Pear(s)
    Endive, and Brie Salad, 17
    Heavenly Fruit Salad with
        Camembert, 174
    Roasted, Arugula and Dandelion
        Salad with, 89
    Russian Fruit and Vegetable Salad,
        183
    and Watercress Salad, 212
Pea(s)
    Black-Eyed, Salad, Portuguese
        Style, 158
    Crunchy Couscous Salad, 177
    Egg, Cheddar, and Rice Salad,
        85
    Green, and Orzo Salad, 102
    Rotelle in Spicy Napoleon Sauce,
        141
    Russian Fruit and Vegetable Salad,
        183
    Russian Potato Salad, 114
    Savory Potato Salad, 37
    Spicy Potato Salad, Country Style,
        81
    St. Basil Macaroni Salad, 168
    St. Scholastica Salad, 41
Pecans
    Boston Salad, 16
    Crunchy Couscous Salad, 177
    Frisée and Bleu d'Auvergne Salad, 19
    New York Columbia County Salad,
        200
    Pear, Endive, and Brie Salad, 17
    Pear and Watercress Salad, 212
    Perugia Fennel Salad, 28
    Smoked Salmon and Apple
        Appetizer, 204
    Tangy Fruit Salad, 172
Penne (pasta)
    Pinoche Pasta Salad, 46
    Salad, 186

Pepper(s)
   All-American Tossed Salad, 101
   Bon Appétit Salad, 67
   Chickpea Salad, 164
   Chickpea Salad, Spanish Style, 176
   Farfalle and Chickpea Salad, 91
   Fava Bean Salad Egyptian Style, 64
   Garden Salad with *Sauce au
      Caviar*, 44
   Gazpacho Salad, 138
   Guacamole Salad, 163
   Japanese Sprout Salad, 11
   Madagascar Date-Nut Salad, 48
   Mango Salad Piquant, 112
   Marinated Roasted, Salad, 29
   Mexican Salad, 199
   Middle Eastern Tabbouleh Salad, 115
   Mixed Jicama Salad, 140
   Orzo and Green Pea Salad, 102
   Penne Salad, 186
   Radicchio and Tomato Salad from
      Venice, 88
   Rigatoni and Broccoli Salad, 187
   Roasted Red, Chicory, and
      Mozzarella Salad, 83
   Roasted Sweet, Salad from the
      Piedmont, 220
   Room-Temperature Red Salad, 216
   *Salade des Crudités*, 145
   *Salade Niçoise*, 135
   *Salade Poitevine*, 207
   Salmon and Cucumber Salad, 73
   Spanish Salad, 136
   Spicy Black Bean Salad, Mexican
      Style, 134
   Spicy Mixed Bean Salad, 18
   St. Basil Macaroni Salad, 168
   St. Fiacre Salad, 148
   Sts. Peter and Paul Salad, 111
   Taramasalata Egg Salad, 72
   Zucchini Salad, Basque Style, 125
Persimmon and Greens Salad, 195
Perugia Fennel Salad, 28
Pesto-Filled Deviled Eggs, 105
Pickled Deviled Egg Salad, 40
Pineapple
   Cabbage, and Apple Slaw, 161
   Royal Fruit Salad, 42
   Tutti-Frutti Salad, 194
Pinoche Pasta Salad, 46

Pole Bean Salad, 166
Pork. *See* Bacon; Ham
Potato(es)
   Baby Beet, and Onion Salad, 162
   and Bean Salad, Sicilian, 121
   Black-Eyed Pea Salad, Portuguese
      Style, 158
   Cold Egg, and Tuna Salad with
      Mustard-Tarragon Dressing, 71
   Russian Fruit and Vegetable Salad,
      183
   Salad, Country Style, Spicy, 81
   Salad, German, 10
   Salad, Russian, 114
   Salad, Savory, 37
   Salad, Sicilian, 54
   Salad, St. John the Baptist, 110
   Salad, Tuscan Style, 74
   Salad Holy Elder Simeon, 191
   Salad Mont-Blanc, 157
   *Salade Nantaise*, 223
   *Salade Rachel*, 94
   South American Bean Salad, 218
   St. Francis Salad, 192
   Tomato Salad, Alsatian Style, 116
Prophet Elijah Lentil Salad, 127
Provençal Mesclun Salad, 92

Q

Quick Belgian-Style Salad, 198

R

Radicchio, 3
   Artichoke Heart Salad, 221
   Fresh Dandelion Salad, 63
   Italian Salad with Cooked
      Dandelion Greens, 107
   Italian Winter Salad, 38
   Orecchiette, and Arugula Salad, 188
   Roasted Red Pepper, Chicory, and
      Mozzarella Salad, 83
   Room-Temperature Red Salad, 216
   Spartan Carrot Salad, 66
   St. Joseph Salad, 58
   and Tomato Salad from Venice, 88
   Venetian Gorgonzola Salad, 32
Radish(es)
   All-American Tossed Salad, 101
   Clementine, Apple, and Spinach
      Salad, 226

Copperfield Salad, 33
   Egg, and Celery Salad with
      Tarragon Sauce, 49
   Israeli Salad, 139
   Italian Mixed Salad, 87
   *Salade Campagnarde*, 208
   *Salade Composée*, 156
   *Salade du Barry*, 93
   St. Anne Salad, 130
   Valle D'Aosta Salad, 103
Rainbow Salad, 193
Raisins
   Cabbage, Apple, and Pineapple
      Slaw, 161
   Chilled Carrot Salad, 82
   Crunchy Couscous Salad, 177
   Mayfair Salad, 30
   Monastery-Style Coleslaw, 222
   Orange and Tangerine Salad, 95
   Peach and Chicory Salad, 150
   St. Benedict Salad, 126
   Stuffed Melon Salad, 131
   Two Cabbages Salad, 14
   Wild Rice and Barley Salad, 35
Raspberry(ies)
   -Scented Vinegar, 236
   Berried Smoked Salmon Salad, 171
   Fruit Relish Salad, 173
   Heavenly Fruit Salad with
      Camembert, 174
   Summer Fruit Platter, 132
Red Beet Salad with Roquefort
   Cheese, 182
Red leaf lettuce, 2
   Cold Egg, Potato, and Tuna Salad
      with Mustard-Tarragon Dressing,
      71
   Roman Mixed Salad, 62
Red oak-leaf lettuce, 2
   Fresh Dandelion Salad, 63
   Garden Salad with *Sauce au
      Caviar*, 44
   Room-Temperature Red Salad, 216
Regina Salad, 147
Rémoulade Dressing, 31
Rémoulade Sauce, 20, 47, 202
Rice
   Egg, and Cheddar Salad, 85
   and Lentil Salad, Mediterranean,
      201

Mexican Salad, 199
St. Benedict Salad, 126
Transfiguration Salad, 137
Wild, and Barley Salad, 35
Rigatoni and Broccoli Salad, 187
Riviera Cantaloupe Salad, 149
Roasted Red Pepper, Chicory, and
    Mozzarella Salad, 83
Roasted Sweet Pepper Salad from the
    Piedmont, 220
Romaine lettuce, 2
    All-American Tossed Salad, 101
    Berried Smoked Salmon Salad, 171
    Bistro Egg Salad, 50
    Caesar Salad, 8
    Italian Summer Salad, 122
    Paradiso Salad, 53
    Regina Salad, 147
Roman Mixed Salad, 62
Room-Temperature Red Salad, 216
Roquefort Cheese
    Dressing, French-Style, 242
    Mayonnaise, 23
    Red Beet Salad with, 182
    Salade au Roquefort, 77
    Salade Picarde, 57
    St. Scholastica Salad, 41
Rotelle in Spicy Napoleon Sauce, 141
Royal Fruit Salad, 42
Russian Fruit and Vegetable Salad,
    183
Russian Potato Salad, 114

S
saints' salads, names of, 59
Salade au Roquefort, 77
Salade Bonne Femme, 109
Salade Camille, 124
Salade Campagnarde, 208
Salade Composée, 156
Salade Croquante, 76
Salade des Crudités, 145
Salade du Barry, 93
Salade Landaise, 189
Salade Nantaise, 223
Salade Niçoise, 135
Salade Nivernaise, 206
Salade Picarde, 57
Salade Poitevine, 207
Salade Rachel, 94

Salade Savoyarde, 167
salads
    preparing, tips for, 4
    salad greens for, 1–4
    types of, 4–6
Salmon
    and Avocado Salad, 52
    and Cucumber Salad, 73
    Paradiso Salad, 53
    Smoked, and Apple Appetizer, 204
    Smoked, Berried Salad, 171
Sevilla Salad, 68
Sicilian Bean and Potato Salad, 121
Sicilian Potato Salad, 54
South American Bean Salad, 218
Spanish Salad, 136
Spartan Carrot Salad, 66
Spicy Balsamic Vinegar, 235
Spicy Black Bean Salad, Mexican
    Style, 134
Spicy Mixed Bean Salad, 18
Spicy Napoleon Sauce, 244
Spicy Oil, 233
Spicy Potato Salad, Country Style, 81
Spicy Spanish Vinaigrette, 238
Spinach, 3
    Ancient Persian Salad, 13
    Baby, and Orange Salad, 15
    Catfish Salad, Greek Style, 106
    Clementine, and Apple Salad, 226
    and Egg Salad, 86
    Fresh Greens and Tuna Salad, 108
    Pinoche Pasta Salad, 46
    Roman Mixed Salad, 62
    Salade Nantaise, 223
    Salade Nivernaise, 206
    Salade Poitevine, 207
    Sevilla Salad, 68
    St. Andrew "The First Called"
        Salad, 209
    St. Joseph Salad, 58
Sprouts. See Bean sprouts
St. Andrew "The First Called" Salad,
    209
St. Anne Salad, 130
St. Basil Macaroni Salad, 168
St. Benedict Salad, 126
St. Cecile Cauliflower Salad, 210
St. Fiacre Salad, 148
St. Francis Salad, 192

St. Hildegarde's Salad, 169
St. Joaquim Salad, 129
St. John the Baptist Potato Salad, 110
St. Joseph Salad, 58
St. Martin Salad, 211
St. Mary Magdalene Salad, 128
St. Michael's Salad, 170
St. Scholastica Salad, 41
Strawberries
    Heavenly Fruit Salad with
        Camembert, 174
    Royal Fruit Salad, 42
    Tutti-Frutti Salad, 194
Sts. Peter and Paul Salad, 111
Stuffed Avocado Salad, 225
Stuffed Melon Salad, 131
Summer Fruit Platter, 132
Summertime Salad, 152

T
Tabbouleh Salad, Middle Eastern,
    115
Tangerine(s)
    and Orange Salad, 95
    Room-Temperature Red Salad, 216
    Tangy Fruit Salad, 172
Tangy Fruit Salad, 172
Taramasalata Egg Salad, 72
Tarragon-Mustard Dressing, 71
Tarragon Sauce, 49
Tarragon Sauce "Classique," 243
Thousand Island Dressing, 240
Tofu Salad, Herbed, 215
Tomato(es)
    All-American Tossed Salad, 101
    Assumpta Salad, 146
    Bistro Egg Salad, 50
    Catfish Salad, Greek Style, 106
    Cherry, and Bulgur Salad, 185
    Chickpea Salad, Spanish Style, 176
    Cooked Fennel Salad, 181
    Costa Brava Egg-and-Tuna Filled,
        117
    Farfalle and Chickpea Salad, 91
    Gazpacho Salad, 138
    Greek-Style Artichoke Salad, 69
    and Green Bean Salad, 179
    Guacamole Salad, 163
    Horiatiki Greek Salad, 155
    Israeli Salad, 139

Tomato(es) *(cont.)*
  Italian Mixed Salad, 87
  Italian Summer Salad, 122
  Macaroni and Green Bean Salad,
    203
  Madrid Mixed Salad, 154
  Mediterranean Lentil and Rice
    Salad, 201
  Middle Eastern Tabbouleh Salad, 115
  Mint-Flavored Fusilli Salad, 118
  Mount St.-Michel Egg Salad, 104
  and Olive Salad from the Lazio, 120
  Onion, and Mozzarella Salad, 143
  Orecchiette, Arugula, and
    Radicchio Salad, 188
  and Parsley Salad, Late-Summer, 165
  Pesto-Filled Deviled Eggs, 105
  Pinoche Pasta Salad, 46
  Pole Bean Salad, 166
  Potato Salad Holy Elder Simeon, 191
  and Radicchio Salad from Venice,
    88
  Regina Salad, 147
  Salad, Alsatian Style, 116
  Salad, Italian, 142
  *Salade Camille*, 124
  *Salade Campagnarde*, 208
  *Salade Composée*, 156
  *Salade des Crudités*, 145
  *Salade Niçoise*, 135
  Spanish Salad, 136
  Spinach and Egg Salad, 86
  St. Cecile Cauliflower Salad, 210
  St. Fiacre Salad, 148
  St. Joaquim Salad, 129
  St. Joseph Salad, 58
  St. Michael's Salad, 170
  St. Scholastica Salad, 41
  Sts. Peter and Paul Salad, 111
  Taramasalata Egg Salad, 72
  Transfiguration Salad, 137
  Tuscan Salad, 123
  Tuscan Stuffed, Salad, 159
  Zucchini Salad, Basque Style, 125
Tonnato Sauce, 70
Transfiguration Salad, 137
Tuna
  -and-Egg Filled Tomatoes, Costa
    Brava, 117
  Ancient Persian Salad, 13

  Cold Egg, and Potato Salad with
    Mustard-Tarragon Dressing, 71
  Eggs Tonnato, 70
  and Fresh Greens Salad, 108
  Madrid Mixed Salad, 154
  *Salade Camille*, 124
  *Salade Niçoise*, 135
  St. Andrew "The First Called"
    Salad, 209
Tuscan Salad, 123
Tuscan Stuffed Tomato Salad, 159
Tutti-Frutti Salad, 194
Two Cabbages Salad, 14

V
Valle D'Aosta Salad, 103
Venetian Gorgonzola Salad, 32
Vinaigrette. *See also individual salad
    recipes*
  with Garlic, 237
  Greek, 106
  with Herbs, 237
  with Mustard, 237
  preparing, 229–230
  Simple, 237
  Spicy Spanish, 238
Vinegar, Basil-Scented, 234
Vinegar, Lemon Verbena–Scented, 234
Vinegar, Raspberry-Scented, 236
Vinegar, Spicy Balsamic, 235

W
Waldorf Salad, 31
Walnuts
  Baby Spinach and Orange Salad, 15
  Crunchy Couscous Salad, 177
  Endive Salad with Blue Cheese, 34
  Peach and Chicory Salad, 150
  Persimmon and Greens Salad, 195
  Potato Salad, Tuscan Style, 74
  *Salade au Roquefort*, 77
  *Salade Picarde*, 57
  Stuffed Melon Salad, 131
  Venetian Gorgonzola Salad, 32
  Waldorf Salad, 31
Watercress, 3
  Ancient Persian Salad, 13
  and Avocado Salad, 184
  Belgian Salad, 12
  Emerald Salad, Indonesian Style, 99

French Mimosa Salad, 56
Fresh Greens and Tuna Salad, 108
Garden Salad with *Sauce au
    Caviar*, 44
Japanese Sprout Salad, 11
Mixed Green Salad Provençal, 144
Monastery Deviled Egg Salad, 21
Mushroom and Avocado Salad,
    98
Oriental Salad, 9
  and Pear Salad, 212
Quick Belgian-Style Salad, 198
Red Beet Salad with Roquefort
    Cheese, 182
Roman Mixed Salad, 62
*Salade Croquante*, 76
*Salade du Barry*, 93
Smoked Salmon and Apple
    Appetizer, 204
St. Martin Salad, 211
Watermelon
  Summer Fruit Platter, 132
  Summertime Salad, 152
Wheat berries
  St. Anne Salad, 130
Wild Rice
  and Barley Salad, 35
  Transfiguration Salad, 137

Y
Yogurt
  Creamy Blue Cheese Dressing, 41
  Crunchy Couscous Salad, 177
  Dressing, 160
  Dutch-Style Egg and Cheese Salad,
    51
  Light Mayonnaise Dressing, 190
  Madagascar Date-Nut Salad, 48
  Mayfair Salad, 30
  Riviera Cantaloupe Salad, 149
  Royal Fruit Salad, 42
  *Salade des Crudités*, 145
  *Salade Savoyarde*, 167
  Spicy Napoleon Sauce, 244
  Summer Fruit Platter, 132
  Tangy Fruit Salad, 172
  Tuscan Stuffed Tomato Salad, 159

Z
Zucchini Salad, Basque Style, 125